ARBITRATION

THE ARBITRATOR AND THE PARTIES

(THEIR RELATIONSHIPS)
(ALLIED TOPICS & JUDICIAL IMMUNITY)

A REVIEW OF A TOPIC THAT AFFECTS EVERY ARBITRATION
AND WHICH IS LIKELY TO BE NEGLECTED
BY THOSE MOST CONCERNED

TOWARDS GREATER UNDERSTANDING

BY

FRANCIS MILLER
Fellow of the Chartered Institute of Arbitrators
Ex-Fellow of the Royal Institution of Chartered Surveyors (1975-94)

Published by Ruthtrek Limited

Published in 1994

by Ruthtrek Limited of 19 High Street, Herne Bay, Kent.

OTHER PUBLICATION BY THE SAME AUTHOR

"ARBITRATION" LIST OF CONTENTS - 1976 to 1985
(The Journal of the Chartered Institute of Arbitrators)

ARBITRATION - Recommendations & Survey
on the
Law and Practice of Arbitration in England & Wales

Building & Civil Engineering - Cost-Value Comparison
(Towards greater understanding)

A catalogue record of his book is available from the British Library

ISBN 0 9514295 3 1

ALL CHARACTER REPRESENTATIONS ARE ENTIRELY FICTITIOUS AND THEIR WORDS ARE SIMPLY THE PRODUCT OF IMAGINATION. HOWEVER, READERS MAY WELL RECOGNISE AN ELEMENT OF TRUTH REFLECTED THEREIN.

QUOTATIONS ARE, OF COURSE, NOT IMAGINARY.

N.B. The text refers to the masculine only in order to avoid the use of clumsy phrases like "his and her" and similar. Hopefully, one day, a neutral pronoun will emerge so that the masculine will not have to embrace the feminine as it does in this publication.

CONTENTS PAGE

The problems that may arise from "a pause" for reflection are compared to the benefits and the situation is likened to the Consumer Arbitration Agreements Act 1988. The discussion revolves around complaints about arbitration procedure as often being unsuitable but unstoppable once started. Having missed the afternoon break, and having concluded that there would be a benefit in "a pause" for reflection, the discussion is closed for another day.

The discussion over the past two days about the understanding of and the relationship between the parties has revealed many problems. Now the discussion centres upon the actual arbitration agreement. The intent of the agreement is considered and also the remedies for failures to comply with the agreement are explored.

The discussion revolves around aspects of consideration and the true basis of an arbitration agreement. The position of the parties is considered in relation to the power of the court to stay under section 4(1) of the Arbitration Act 1950. And, Lord Diplock's concept of mutual obligations is again reviewed just before a break for lunch.

S... opens the afternoon discussion with a suggestion that an arbitration agreement is simply a fiduciary arrangement. The fiduciary aspect of the agreement is debated at length and it is concluded that, with some reservations, the true nature of the agreement has been found. In addition, a reference is made to arbitration as being a "privilege." The afternoon break has been missed and the discussion ends for the day.

The discussion moves on to the relationship between the arbitrator and the parties. The fiduciary element is considered along with the problems of the arbitrator being appointed and accepting the appointment. The problem of

INTRODUCTION

A serious subject treated like a fiction story, that will never do!

I hope you will not agree. I hope you will find that the principal text is a good-read and that in reading it you are able to recall colleagues who have spoken in such terms. I hope that some of the observations will make you chuckle a little and that others will make you feel a little cross - not with me, but with the characters portrayed. Mostly, I hope that you will find your head nodding in agreement - not necessarily with the conclusions, but with the fact that so much uncertainty still remains to be clarified. Uncertainty about issues which should be the solid foundation upon which all arbitration is founded: namely, the relationship between the parties themselves and between the parties and the arbitrator.

The text starts off as a dialogue between four people. It is followed by associated comments and pertinent quotations extracted from published material. The object which I had in mind was this: That having read the dialogue, the reader's thoughts will be activated into believing that more research into this important aspect of arbitration is needed. If that belief can be instigated, then I hope that the comments and quotations provided will assist with further research. So, please read the whole dialogue first.

The dialogue is intended to be part only of a wider discussion. The characters have already taken part in discussing some other issues and now they turn their attention to the topic which forms the title of this book. These other issues may form the basis of a further publication. For example, it is intended that a subsequent book in this series will deal with the definition and the philosophy of arbitration. The point is this: That the discussion is never complete, it is only ever part of a larger scene.

In the present dialogue, the characters start off by having a "dig" at the lack of interest in arbitration shown by Members of Parliament, then they proceed on by firstly trying to identify the subject of their discussions and how best to consider the subject. The discussion takes place over five consecutive days: a complete luxury which is denied to most people. If ever there is a five day conference, every one expects - generally - that a very wide range of topics will be covered. There never seems to be enough time to discuss a single topic for five days, or longer; everyone is too busy. Perhaps that is why so many aspects of arbitration are left in a state of continual uncertainty.

The five days are each divided into four sessions of some one and a quarter hours each. The whole tenor of the discussion is leisurely; i.e., talk, reflection and more talk. The dialogue does not, of course, take place at reading speed; a reader will cover the whole five days in just a few hours.

I have purposely created a morning coffee break, a lunch break and an afternoon break. This provides an opportunity for discussion to take place which is not recorded in the text; that discussion is left to the reader's imagination. Of course, from my point of view, if any reader tells me that I have left some important issues out of the dialogue, I will reply that the point was discussed during one of the breaks. Nevertheless, I shall be pleased for any views about content, both in omission or in commission, to be sent to me via the publishers.

I respectfully suggest that nothing written, which is complete in any absolute sense, would ever stir the reader's own imagination. In my opinion, part of the greatest value of any written work is the gaps which are filled by the reader's own knowledge and imagination; so, I do not claim that this work is complete or definitive. I want it to be a catalyst producing a greater understanding. I wish only that it were really possible to be informed about the gap-filling and the alternatives fleshed out in the mind of a reader.

Why did I choose these particular characters?

Three of the characters require no explanation. **A...**, **B...** and **C...** being an arbitrator, a barrister and a commercial man respectively. All have considerable experience of arbitration. The arbitrator, with a non-lawyer background, having been an expert and then subsequently an arbitrator. The barrister, having been an advocate and also an arbitrator. The commercial man being a business man who has faced arbitration many times as a disputant. The main point about these three people is this: That in spite of their obvious knowledge about disputes and arbitrations, they are not certain about the issues being discussed. Or, perhaps I should say, they are all certain about the uncertainty surrounding the issues. Of course, if I misrepresent the people whom the characters represent, then I am able to say they are individuals and not every individual knows everything. But if any reader from one of the classes of those whom the characters represent is able to come forward and tell me that he knows the precise position on these issues, then, he will not only disabuse me, he will considerably assist the whole [perhaps with the exception of himself] entourage of the arbitration business. If, of course, I am the only one who needs to be disabused of my thinking, the sooner I know the better.

The use of **S...** and **P...** is either a good idea or a bad one; dependent upon one's line of thinking. Greek scholars may well condemn such a flippant use of great names.

I have been greatly impressed by reading the dialectic treatment of topical issues arising over two thousand five hundred years ago. Some of the issues then discussed are still being discussed and are still not settled matters. But of more direct importance, it seemed to me that one must first have something to say and, secondly, make it a good read, otherwise the whole exercise is wasted time. As to the second, I have found that a dialectic handling of a topic helps to cultivate the right frame of mind in the reader; so that the writer can get his point across. Had I written the same thing without reference to **S... & P...**, then some readers would surely say that he tried to copy the great masters and has done so but very poorly. Whereas, by taking the bold approach, I pay homage to the masters, and no one would expect me to be their equivalent. I am more content to pay homage and to offer a sub-standard representation, than to have tried to achieve the equivalent on the pretence that it was origination. There is another aspect. I am anxious to high-light the fact that most things which we discuss today have been discussed for thousands of years and much evidence exists to prove it. Yet, still there is a tendency to believe that things which are being wrought today are the product of original thinking. At the highest level of acclaim, I think the most we can ever achieve is to present - as the moviemakers say - a "new angle."

If what I have written is a "new angle" on an old matter, then I shall be satisfied. I shall be even more satisfied if, through wider debate, we can clarify our thinking on these topics, just a little.

Francis Miller

ACKNOWLEDGEMENTS

My most grateful thanks to the many colleagues who have expressed encouragement and who have, by their comments over the years, given me the confidence to explore the subject in this unconventional way. In particular, I thank His Honour Brian Clapham (retired Judge and experienced arbitrator) for reading the draft and making many valuable suggestions about context and the text generally. I am also pleased to acknowledge the concerns expressed by Kerry Harding (Secretary of the Chartered Institute of Arbitrators) about the absence of a statement identifying the underlying philosophy for arbitration and also the absence of a definition of arbitration. Kerry Harding's concerns were based primarily on the fact that - without a definition and a philosophical statement - a reader, lacking in knowledge of arbitration, may gain the impression that the dialogue emphasises "self-interest" and that the characters adopt a "defensive" standpoint on the issues of judicial immunity. These concerns have encouraged me to make a note in the Introduction about my intention to write a sequential book dealing in greater detail with these issues. However, Kerry Harding, as always, has been supportive of my efforts to analyse issues of importance in arbitration and his encouragement is much appreciated.

**IF SOCRATES WERE ALIVE TODAY
WOULD PLATO HAVE WRITTEN THIS?**

AUTOMATIST : FRANCIS MILLER

THE DIALOGUE

THE ARBITRATOR AND THE PARTIES
(Their relationships)

The persons present

A...	An arbitrator
B...	A barrister
C...	A commercial man
S...	Discussion co-ordinator
P...	Note-taker

[PLEASE READ THE BRIEF INTRODUCTION FIRST]

1 **S...** : I'm thankful that there is a good fire today, I was rather cold yesterday. Where I've come from it is usually much warmer . . . and dryer.

P... : Quite so, but the discussion of yesterday kept our minds off the cold. I'm looking forward to today's topic.

S... : The three MPs are late. I thought they would be early.

C... : I don't think they're coming.

S... : They seemed very keen, yesterday.

C... : Yes, they were. When they were talking about maternity allowances, social security issues, expanding the economy, etc., they were the biggest talkers. Didn't you notice how they lost interest when **P...** said that he was looking forward to the discussion on arbitration.

S... : No. I was too busy listening.

2 **A...** : It's rather odd when you think about it. The House of Commons and the House of Lords is brimming over with lawyers and yet so few of them are interested in topics like arbitration.

C... : No votes in it, that's why!

S... : How do you know that MPs are not interested in arbitration? I distinctly heard them mention the word several times yesterday. They frequently said things like this: "That problem should be sent to arbitration," or "No one should be allowed to disrupt daily life without first going to arbitration."

C... : MPs just use the term, "arbitration," as a word. They treat it like a panacea. They think that if they say the magic word, "ARBITRATION," the problems will all fade away.

S... : My dear **C...**, that's a bit cynical for a man of industry, isn't it?

C... : I wish I could admit to being cynical . . . but, I'm sorry to say, it seems to me to be the truth of the matter.

B... : As a lawyer, myself, I sorry to say that I'm inclined to agree with our good friend, C....

C... : At last, I find there is an issue where the lawyers and commercial men are on common ground . . . at least, two of them, anyway.

S... : But, I return to my question, how do you know that MPs are not interested in arbitration?

A... : A reference book called, "Dod's Parliamentary Companion," which has been published regularly for over 160 years, tells me so.

S... : Tell me more.

A... : This reference book, and I refer to the one hundred and seventy third edition, 1992, lists down all the stated interests of MPs and members of the House of Lords. Not one MP expresses an interest in arbitration. And only one member of the House of Lords expresses a specific interest.

B... : Who's that?

A... : Lord Hacking. He lists an interest in Commercial Law and International Arbitration.

S... : Well, my dear **A...**, that seems fairly conclusive, but I have a feeling that many MPs . . . or members of the Upper House . . . would regard something like arbitration as being only incidental to their main interest . . .

P... : Do you want me to keep a note of all these incidental discussions or shall I wait until we get into the real issues?

S... : I must ask you to note everything, because we will not know what the real issues are until after we have completed our discussion. Indeed, it may be of crucial importance that MPs do not spend sufficient time on the mundane issues of every-day arbitration. Perhaps that's where the core of the problem lies . . . but let's not prejudge the issue. Let's leave the matter of MPs' interest in arbitration to one side and get on with the main topic.

A... : I agree, but it does seem a pity that our three MPs will not be with us.

C... : I agree. I don't know very much about these things. But I know what arbitration is, I know it's often very expensive and it sometimes takes ages to get a decision. My lawyers are always telling me that they are working wonders on my behalf, even when I lose!

B... : I think our friend feigns his lack of knowledge. He has been involved in more arbitrations than most lawyers . . . and, dare I say it, most arbitrators.

S... : Be that as it may. Let's get on. Let us, first, ask **A...** to high-light the issue for our present discussion. Come on **A...**, set down the points you were on about yesterday.

A... : Yesterday . . . well . . . the point I made was about all the uncertainty concerning the status of the arbitrator and his relationship with the parties. Is it contractual? If not, what is it?

S... : I don't specifically recall you speaking about contractual arrangements. You did say that you were growing in your concern about the issue of judicial immunity, recovery of fees and the appointing system for arbitrators.

A... : Yes, I did, but I regard them all to be problems arising out of the uncertainty about the relationship between the arbitrator and the parties.

C... : I must say that I always thought that arbitrators had the same judicial immunity as a judge. I can recall one arbitrator who was useless, I wouldn't have paid him a penny if I had my way. But when I told my solicitor that we should take action to recover unnecessary expense, she told me that I didn't stand a chance and that I should pay the arbitrator and get the award. As it happened, when I paid his fee and got the award it was in my favour and the other side had to pay his fees in the end; and a good part of my cost as well . . . served them right. But, if I had been the other side, I would have sued the arbitrator. My solicitor simply said that the result had turned out as she had anticipated, and that was that.

S... : My dear friends . . . if we are going to have a meaningful discussion and reach some conclusions we must not allow ourselves the luxury of carefree discussion. We must take each issue separately and find out what we know already and then see if we can agree upon a way forward or, at least, see where we disagree. If we manage to find the answer on each separate point we may be able to gather together all our answers and point to a general way forward for arbitration. Let's decide where to begin. You are the experts on arbitration, I know nothing . . . as I get older, I get better at framing the questions but, sadly, as is clearly evidenced from what you say, we cannot seem to find answers. We must always try, but we must not deceive ourselves in believing that there are answers that will stand the test of all time. However, if we can find some answers that are relevant to the present time or just some specific dispute we may have made some progress.

C... : I grow impatient for answers to questions that should be simple to deal with. I should have been a politician. I would have put things in order. If the politicians ran the country like I run my business, everything would be all right.

A... : I too grow impatient over all these matters. Surely some of these issues are simple to deal with. They just require a decision one way or the other, and then we shall all know where we stand.

S... : If only life was so simple. I can tell you that over two thousand five hundred years ago people in ancient Greece were discussing problems very similar to your own. There were some sound ideas around at that time, but still the issues cry out for debate and fresh ideas.

B... : As a lawyer . . . .

C... : As a lawyer, you revel in all the uncertainty. It's all money to you.

3 **S...** : I don't think it will do much good to speak as you do . . . although I have to say that lawyers received the same comments all those years ago in ancient Greece . . . nothing much seems to have changed.

B... : Am I to be an outcast, when I thought I was amongst friends?

A... : No, my old friend, its just banter.

S... : Come, then . . . what is to be the first topic?

A... : It is a case of the chicken and the egg, as to which is to come first. If we resolved the business of the relationship between the arbitrator and the parties we may resolve all the other issues. On the other hand if we resolve each of the other issues we may have also resolved the issue of the relationship.

S... : From what you have just said, I believe that we must deal with individual issues. I understand the dilemma which you have placed before us, but we have got to start somewhere. It would boost our confidence if we could start with the simplest problem first, so what will it be?

C... : I'm sure I don't know, I must leave it up to the experts.

A... : It is really difficult to find a problem which is simple to resolve. It is self-evident that if a problem is simple to resolve, then it is not a problem.

S... : That's a good point, but it is not a good reply to the point that I made. I did not say, "simple," I said, "the simplest problem." There is a big difference.

A... : I'm sorry, obviously I was not listening to your every word.

C... : Well, there you have it in a nutshell. An arbitrator who doesn't listen to what he is being told.

B... : It seems that we are all going to have to keep on our toes and pay attention. **S...** has the both the skill to ask the right question and the memory to remember what he has asked. And, dear old **C...** has the lively mind of a man who has lived in the real world of commerce. As to **A...** and myself, we shall have to keep our wits about us, else we shall expose our failings.

A... : I started off my career as a . . . .

S... : Humbleness is always a good stating point in any discussion. As for our good friend **C...**, he will have made a valuable contribution to the debate if he does nothing more than remind us of our shortcomings. Now let's find the starting point, the simplest problem.

P... : I have arranged for coffee to be brought in, it should be here soon, would this be a good point to break off?

S... : Oh! Just as we were on the point of starting. But, I agree.

[POST COFFEE BREAK]

THE AGREEMENT OF THE PARTIES

S... : Judging by your lively discussions over coffee, we are not likely to find an easy starting point, are we?

4 **B...** : I am sorry to say that the more we talk about it, the more of a problem it becomes. Oh dear! At one stage in my career, I thought that arbitration was so straightforward. We had only one real reference book, it was called "Russell on Arbitration." Very few people actually read it. It was a bit like the Bible, not many read it but it's always there if you wanted to . . . Ah! Those were the days.

C... : Well, perhaps that's the answer. Stop talking about it and just get on with it. That's the problem with the world today, everyone keeps talking and talking instead of getting on and doing things.

5 **A...** : Our friend does have a point, I've often said that if the parties just trusted in the arbitrator and left everything to his discretion, then everything would be all right. If we could have the power to decide *ex aequo et bono* and if we could do what we believed to be right in all the circumstances . . . .

B... : Well, my good friend, I did not expect to hear you say that, I think you must be getting old. You'll remember our discussion years ago when you were acting as a lay advocate and an expert. All those unkind things you said about arbitrators who did not follow established principles of law and procedure . . . .

S... : Hold on, my good friends. I can see that discussing arbitration is like opening a can of worms. We must be very careful. We must open the can with great care and pull out one worm only, examine it in great detail, mark it, and put it back. Then select another.

C... : I thought that all worms looked the same.

S... : I must be careful that I don't lead the discussion into a wildlife debate. Now lets decide upon our first issue . . . even if it is not the simplest, we must start somewhere.

C... : Why not put all the issues down on a piece of paper and put them into a hat, pull one out and whatever it is, we'll start there.

A... : That sounds good enough.

B... : All right, but are we going to limit the issues to the main broad topics or take subsidiary issues as well. It may be a problem if we take out two subsidiary issues about different topics, it may . . . .

S... : My dear friends, let me put a point to you. You have spoken about the relationship between the arbitrator and the parties, matters of public policy, judicial immunity, powers of the arbitrator and a whole lot more. But what about the relationship between the parties themselves, what about that?

B... : Oh! That's quite simple. They just enter into a simple arbitration agreement, which requires no special words. There is no problem in that area.

S... : Simple beginnings, long term problems, is my response to your observation.

6 **B...** : Leaving aside special laws concerning consumers, it could not be simpler. It is only the choice of whether you do it or whether you don't.

S... : Anything which can be started off with but little thought has enormous potential for long-term problems. Take life itself. . . . Such a simple beginning - even made the product of pleasure - yet the consequences of creating a new life without careful planning can be disastrous. If all of us gave more thought to all things created with simple beginnings, we would have to give less thought to those great provisions and resources of the world; over which we have so little control.

A... : What, you mean like third-world starvation, the ozone layer depletion, consumption of natural resources, etc., etc. . . . Well, that's a bit heavy for a discussion about arbitration agreements isn't it? Dear **S...** you are doing the same as you say we're doing: expanding the topics and not keeping to the issues.

S... : I don't think so my dear friend. The whole business of disputes is just as much a problem to mankind as the sad things about which you have spoken.

7 **B...** : True enough, I accept that the number of lawyers worldwide is testimony to what you have just said. The only places in the world where lawyers are not a major force in society are, in fact, the places where people

are suffering some other major problem, like starvation. You are right, my friend. The relationship between the parties is a good starting point. But . . . I do assure you . . . it really is a very simple point. However, we shall dispose of it quickly and it may help us on our way forward. On the other hand, if it is not so simple, well . . . well 'tis right that it marks our beginning.

THE AGREEMENT OF THE PARTIES: THEIR RELATIONSHIP

8 **S...** : Our dear friend **B...** will help us if he tells us about the legal position of parties about to enter into an arbitration agreement.

B... : It is quite simple really. Two or more parties enter into a simple agreement to have their differences resolved by arbitration. And, having done so, then they are bound to resolve their differences by arbitration.

S... : Well, my dear **B...**, I must say that I expected to be listening to you for a much longer period.

B... : To have added more to what I have said would be simply unnecessary padding out, otiose. It is really as simple as I have stated.

S... : So these people just say to each other, "Let us resolve our differences by arbitration," and that is that.

9 **B...** : No, not quite. If they just say it to each other, then it will be an oral agreement and such an agreement will not have the support of the Arbitration Acts. The parties will only have the benefit of a type of common law arbitration which would be fraught with difficulties. It would be a very difficult matter to enforce any award made under an oral agreement because the agreement would have to be proven together with award. It would be much worse than trying to enforce any simple oral contract because the party trying to enforce the award would not even have any evidence of performance under the agreement other than the award itself and the events leading up to it. For example, if there were an oral agreement to build a wall for a reasonable sum of money, at least there would be the evidence of the wall itself if the dispute was only about the money. Of course, it would be much more difficult to prove that an oral contract existed if the wall had not been built. And, there again . . . .

S... : I'm sorry to butt in, but I can see that the agreement to arbitrate should be in writing. Oral agreements on anything are always difficult when a dispute arises, so it would not be wise to have an oral agreement to resolve a dispute, that's for sure. But that raises another issue and that is this: You, my dear **B...**, are a lawyer and would be expected to know about these things. How would a man in the street know what to do? How would he know that it was unwise to enter into an oral agreement to arbitrate?

B... : Well, I don't suppose he would. I . . . .

S... : I'm sorry to butt in again, but this is an important point. Let me explain it by way of an example. You mentioned about the building of a wall, and that will form the basis of my example. When one party asks another to build a wall, we can assume that he does so because he believes that the other party is capable of building the required wall and has all the resources to do so. Likewise, the party who is to build the wall has a right to assume that the other party - the customer - has the money to pay for the work. So we can say that both parties are, or should be, fully aware of their respective obligations under the agreement, be it an oral agreement or an agreement in writing.

B... : That is obvious, it hardly needs a mention.

10 **S...** : Quite. But what I have been told about arbitration leads me to believe that the parties may well enter into an arbitration agreement without either, or any, of them having the faintest idea about arbitration or their respective rights and obligations. Or, indeed, whether they should enter into an oral agreement or a written agreement.

A... : I believe that to be the case generally. From my own experience, most parties only discover what arbitration is all about after they are deeply engaged in the arbitration procedure. Many of them say, "Never again." Unless, of course, they are like **C...** who is greatly experienced at being in dispute and his like are few in number.

B... : When people are in dispute and when they have to turn to arbitration or, indeed, litigation they are more than likely to say, "Never again." However, that does not mean to say that they can dispense with the procedure, if they need it, whether they know anything about it or not.

S... : So, the situation seems to be much worse that even I originally feared. None of you are coming forward with the counter-argument that parties do know what they are doing when they select arbitration. You are simply accepting that generally the parties do not know much about arbitration.

C... : I believe that I can endorse what you have just said. I knew nothing about arbitration until I found myself involved in an arbitration as a respondent. And, moreover, I do not think that the claimant knew very much either, even though he was represented by his "family" lawyer. Of course, as has been said, I know a lot more now. But, it is often the case that the other side in my disputes knows nothing about what is involved.

S... : Well my dear friends, would I be going too far if I said that, for practical purposes, most people who enter into arbitration agreements know very little about arbitration? Or, at least, knew very little about it when they were involved in their first arbitration.

C... : I agree.

A... : I too, am bound to agree.

B... : I agree, but that is the inevitable consequence of any dispute resolution procedure, be it litigation, arbitration, conciliation, mediation, mini-trial, what have you.

11 **S...** : I am intrigued by the expression mini-trial, but I must discipline myself and ask **P...** simply to make a note of it for a further discussion, else, we shall, I fear, get side-tracked.

12 **P...** : I have made a note, but I can see that a reference appears already under the topic of ADR which forms part of **B...**'s notes. ADR stands for "Alternative dispute resolution."

S... : It is so easy to get side-tracked, so let me state again that we are all agreed upon this: Most people who enter into arbitration agreements know very little about arbitration.

"AGREED."

13 **S...** : So, one needs no training, or knowledge, whatsoever, in order to enter into an arbitration agreement.

B... : That's about the measure of it.

S... : My dear **C...**, you are an experienced commercial man who is never likely to enter into anything unless you know what you are doing, so why did you enter into your first arbitration agreement?

14 **C...** : The arbitration clause was just included within a standard form of contract which my company had been using for some years. No one even knew it was there until the other party asked us to concur in the appointment of an arbitrator. We told them what they could do with themselves and the next thing we knew was that an arbitrator had been appointed by the

president of the trade body and that was that; we were suddenly taking part in an arbitration. Our legal advisers said that there was nothing we could do about it. I can tell you it . . . .

S... : I don't wish to stop your story which I am sure will make for some lively discussion when we break for food. But you must have known about the arbitration agreement within your standard contract.

C... : In a way, yes. In so far that some one within my group would have known something about it, even if only very little. But, the details of such agreements do not seem very important in relation to all the other obligations and rights covered by the contract; which obligations and rights, if undertaken properly, will not give rise to any dispute. And, most people, do not expect to be in dispute with each other when they enter into a contract. It's a little bit like having insurance for fire damage. No one really expects to have a fire, so no one reads all the terms of the fire insurance policy until a fire occurs, except - of course - the lawyers who put the terms together in the first place. When a fire does occur, that's when all the experts crawl out from their hiding places in the hopes of earning big fees out of the disaster; and their hopes are usually fulfilled. Likewise, litigation and arbitration, and all the other methods of dispute resolution. All forms of dispute resolution are potential earnings for the experts, so no form of dispute resolution will ever be economical for the people in dispute; that's a fact of life.

15

B... : Dear old **C...** is really becoming more cynical as he grows older.

C... : And to justify it, my dear **B...**, you are growing richer and richer as each year passes by.

A... : I am humbled by my relative poverty compared to both **B...** and **C....**

16 **S...** : I believe that **C...** is quite right to make the points so firmly because it concentrates our thinking. It is not possible to educate an entire nation about all the things that they ought to know, so there is no real way of overcoming lack of general knowledge on such an important topic as dispute resolution. I believe that we must just accept things as being as they are; they cannot be changed, at least not in the short-term. However, it is much better that we know how things are than to believe that people know generally about things when in fact they don't.

A... : I agree. I believe that it is better to assume that no one other than the experts know about arbitration procedure and the risks involved. But where does that take us?

S... : The recognition of a simple truth takes us all the way that we wish to go, for we can go no further than discovering the truth of the matter.

A... : I agree. But how does that help us deal with the issue of the relationship between the parties?

S... : I think that we might adjourn at this point and have our lunch, which I see is on the table.

[POST LUNCH]

THE RELATIONSHIP BETWEEN PEOPLE IN DISPUTE AND THEIR POTENTIAL UNAWARENESS ABOUT ARBITRATION

S... : My dear friends, there is clearly a dilemma which must be faced, namely: (a) Is it in the interest of arbitration procedure generally and of the individuals themselves to allow people to enter into arbitration agreements if it is quite clear that they may trigger off a chain of events about which they know nothing? Or, (b) should anyone be free to be reckless enough to do that which they please regardless of the effect to themselves and to a recognised dispute procedure? We must not make any mistake by using loose words. It is a most reckless act to agree that all differences that may arise shall be resolved by arbitration, if in fact, one does not know what arbitration
17 is.

B... : I'm placed in an awkward position, because I don't like the way that S... has set down the options and yet I cannot instantly replace them with ones that cause me less concern. The stark choice between the two, when put in that way, is - to say the least - a shock to my normal thought process. I have never questioned arbitration in this way before. I have always accepted its procedure as coming into existence . . . well . . . as a matter of fact, regardless of the position of the parties. My position has been this: Parties got themselves into a dispute, they have an arbitration agreement, that is that, so now they must see it through to a conclusion and face up to the consequences.

C... : So, B... must give the affirmative to option (b) to keep faith with his existing views.

B... : Quite so. But I cannot at this instant do that and that concerns me. For my entire working life as a barrister, I have to admit that such thoughts which we have arrived at today have not entered my head.

S... : At least, my dear **B...**, you are being plainly honest. How about you, **A...**, you are keeping very quiet?

A... : I'm thinking.

S... : Yes, but what are you thinking, please speak out, you are amongst friends.

18 **A...** : Well, I need more time to respond. I'm sure you will understand that as an arbitrator, usually the first time I ever see people in dispute is when the arbitration is under way. And, although - as I have said - I believe most people never knew what they were letting themselves in for, I have never really thought about that situation; beyond the simple fact that they don't know much about it but they are now before me and it is up to me to deal with the arbitration as best I can.

S... : I had no idea that the dilemma which I posed would cause such difficulty. Perhaps I could suggest that if the affirmative is given to option (b), then the position is much the same as you have all understood it to be at present and thus there would be no change. Whereas, if the negative is given to option (a) then no one should be allowed to entered into an arbitration agreement without some form of counselling or guidance; and that would cause havoc to the present situation. However, it would mean that arbitration generally would benefit enormously because no one would be involved in arbitration who did not know what it was all about.

C... : Well, gentlemen, **S...** has cut a fine distinction for us, so let us choose. From my experience, I would give the negative to option (a) and prevent anyone from settling a dispute by arbitration unless they were properly briefed about the procedure, including responsibility about costs and delays and the like.

19 **A...** : That would kill arbitration stone-dead.

C... : What if it did? The only losers would be the arbitrators and the experts.

S... : Are you telling me that if people really understood what arbitration was all about, then no one would want arbitration and the procedure would fade away and fall into disuse?

A... : Well, something like that, I suppose.

S... : Then, my good friends, I believe we should stop our discussion right now, because if that is the case, then arbitration should be allowed to fade away. It is a peculiar type of dispute resolution procedure that only survives on the foundation that people in dispute are lured into using it simply because they know nothing about it.

B... : I feel that I am being drawn down to a conclusion which I know is unacceptable, yet I cannot fight against it with any form of logic, except to say that if people want to be so reckless then that is their problem, but I know - in reality - I must never say that. Although that is the simple truth by which I have lived my whole professional life.

20 **S...** : Then . . . shall we close the discussion and call arbitration an unwanted procedure that has now had its day? Let us discuss another topic like . . . what did you call it **P...** ? Was it ADR?

21 **P...** : Come, come, **S...**, stop this melodrama and let's move to the happy ending straightaway. Just look at the glum faces of our good friends **A...** and **B....** Only **C...** seems to see the funny side of it all. Arbitration has survived for thousands of years in spite of the regular interference of man's intuition and it will continue to survive as it adapts continually to the ways of commerce and to life generally. So let's move forward.

22 **S...** : Yes that is true, but I give fair warning that it will not survive effectively
unless the people who use it understand it. In ancient Greece, everyone who
used arbitration, or the neighbourhood courts as they were termed, knew
precisely what arbitration was all about. But then, everyone was expected to
get involved in all the goings-on of the community. However, communities
are much bigger these days and effective means must be found to prevent
people from being drawn into a procedure for the resolution of disputes
which they do not understand. It is my own belief that people will prefer
arbitration more, the more they know about it and the less they are forced
into using it by default. And, if my belief is wrong, then arbitration is no use
23 to anyone in any event. Litigation is the real default procedure whereby
people can be dragged, as reluctant parties, to answer to the wrongs with
which they have been charged at the unilateral motion of another individual.
And, litigation should be the only default procedure: a procedure, supervised
by the state, continually in place, ready to deal with all those matters that
parties cannot resolve of their own accord by agreement or, at least, agreed
procedures. No other procedure should ever be a default procedure except
by the willing consent of the parties in dispute; and how can anyone conclude
that there is willing consent when the parties, one, both or all, do not even
understand what the procedure is all about?

24 **B...** : I'm glad that you have kept the topic alive. On reflection, I can see what you are getting at. In recent times, we have all tried to make arbitration the default procedure for the resolution of all disputes, regardless of the knowledge or desires of the parties. Now we are suffering the backlash. As I speak, I feel like a convert. I feel that no one must ever be dragged, kicking and screaming, into arbitration. They must all come by consent; consent based on knowledge and understanding and not on ignorance. I feel that I have seen the light. But I expect that more careful thought will bring me back to reality.

A... : I too feel that the right course is as you have said. I remember some time ago that Lord Diplock said something about mutual consent of the parties. He was greatly criticised for his observations by many other judges and senior lawyers. He was rather rubbished for his views. I wish I could think of the case.

25 **B...** : I am reminded that I too was one of those who spoke a little unkindly about Lord Diplock at the time. I am reluctant to say so, but perhaps he was right. I remember the words quite well, they are imprinted on my mind. He spoke about the mutual obligations of the parties in private arbitration. For example, he spelt out that the respondent, as well as the claimant, is under a mutual obligation to join in applying to the arbitrator for appropriate directions to put an end to delay. My own position was that if the mutual obligation existed in respect of putting an end to delay, then the mutual obligation extended to every aspect of procedure, leaving only the substance of the dispute as being the contentious issue. I did not like the idea of mutual obligations because it was alien to all my training.

A... : But what was the case?

B... : It was the *Bremer Vulcan* case.

C... : Well, there you have it. Old Diplock was a wise old bird. One thing is for certain. You can't have mutual obligations if the parties have no idea what the obligations are and no idea what arbitration is all about prior to getting involved in it. No wonder people fight so fiercely for their corner . . . when they only learn about the obligations and the rules of play once they are standing in the ring and the fighting begins.

S... : I think that this is a good time to conclude for the day. I can see by the bewildered look on **B...**'s face that we are not going to make further progress today. For my part, I do not believe that the lapse of some time will destroy the conclusion which I have reached. Indeed, I believer further time will strengthen the case for the informed, as opposed to the ignorant, chooser of arbitration. Let's go home and sleep on the issue and start afresh tomorrow.

B... : I could put some thoughts to you right now.

C... : I'm for hearing them tomorrow.

A... : Me too.

P... : If **B...** was writing instead of me, I'm sure we would have concluded some while ago. Shall we say 10.00 a.m. tomorrow gentlemen? . . . Then that's what it will be.

[10.00 a.m. ON THE MORROW]

S... : I see that **B...** is looking full of confidence this morning. His looks signal that some research was undertaken last night, whilst the rest of us took to rest and sleep.

B... : Yes, I did some deep thinking following our departure. Like a lot of ideas, it all seems very well until careful study is undertaken . . . then. . . . Well, to put my thoughts bluntly, the problems of implementation are insurmountable. There is no way that it could be done. None whatsoever.

S... : My dear **B...**, you sound very confident, but may I start by asking you all this question: Are we all still agreed that option (a) should have the negative? You remember that option (a) was this: Is it in the interest of arbitration procedure generally and of the individuals themselves to allow people to enter into arbitration agreements if it is quite clear that they may trigger off a chain of events about which they know nothing? . . . But, before you answer, I wish to adopt some different words. I thought that **B...** summed up the position very well yesterday and on reflection I believe his choice of words to be better; in so far that we do not have to keep referring to the positive with a negative. If I recall his words correctly, he said: "No one must ever be dragged, kicking and screaming, into arbitration. They must all come by consent; consent based on knowledge and understanding and not on ignorance." Am I correct?

B... : Yes, I did say that, but . . . .

S... : It is only your choice of words that I have repeated, you will be free to defeat you own words if you so wish. Now can we agree that those words express our true beliefs?

C... : It's O.K. by me.

26 **A...** : I have thought about it all very carefully, and like **B...**, I spent some considerable time going over the issue last night. I am quite satisfied that we have touched upon a core problem and I believe the sentiment expressed is absolutely correct, but there are bound to be problems. What happens if the respondent does not want to answer to the claim and pleads ignorance about arbitration and . . . .

S... : One thing at a time please. It would be a significant step forward to identify the real issue and define it; even if subsequently we cannot do anything about it. But I am not that pessimistic, although I suppose experience tells me that I ought to be.

A... : We must live in the real world. It does not matter a single jot how good a concept is, if it cannot be instigated.

27 **S...** : Quite so. But the real world is telling us that there is something fundamentally wrong with arbitration today because there is a great deal of complaint about the procedure, the cost, the uncertainty, the delay, etcetera. So please, one step at a time, can we agree upon the sentiment expressed and also upon the words used to express the sentiment.

C... : I've already agreed.

A... : I agree to the sentiment, but I do not like using the words "kicking and screaming." I would prefer this: No one must ever be drawn, reluctantly or unknowingly, into arbitration. They must all come by consent; consent based on knowledge and understanding and not on ignorance."

28 **B...** : It seems to me to be inevitable that many people will be drawn into arbitration reluctantly, even though they willingly consented, even though they had complete knowledge of the arbitration process. So we cannot use that expression. I agree about the concept of "unknowingly" because no one should ever be involved "unknowingly" in an arbitration. In any event, as arbitration is only ever the result of an agreement, how could anyone be involved unknowingly, except possibly as a result of fraud; in which case the agreement would not be enforceable. And, if you say "unknowingly" on the basis that the party did not read the contract which was agreed and signed, then you will be on very dangerous ground. Very dangerous, indeed.

S... : You have certainly demolished **A...**'s amendment. Perhaps you would prefer to keep your own words "kicking and screaming"?

B... : Those words were merely demonstrative expressions, which flowed out at the time of general discussion. They have no specific meaning in the context of drafting a resolution. In fact, they are simply tautologous expressions emphasising the word "consent."

A... : You may have a situation where someone consents under pressure; as in the case of acquiescence. So I do believe that consent needs some qualification.

S... : Consent is already qualified in a sense, because **B...** said, "Consent based on knowledge and understanding and not on ignorance."

B... :How about this: All disputants must come to arbitration willingly by consent; based on knowledge and understanding and not ignorance?

S... : There may still be room for improvement, but let us not debate the words any further. Are we now all agreed that these words express our sentiments?

C... : Everyone picks at words, to me these words say exactly the same as those I agreed to some time ago. Yes, of course, I agree.

A... : So do I.

B... : Agreed.

S... : Excellent. Now my dear **B...**, you will now wish to defeat your own words and argue against them.

B... : No. I have already said that I agreed. Following yesterday, I have accepted the principle. Prior to yesterday, I would have held that the only requirement for arbitration was the consent of the parties. That is still, of
29 course, the law. But, I am now convinced that arbitration is a hopeless procedure if the parties are themselves ignorant of its workings. I can imagine arbitration in olden times. The man on the quay-side, hoping to catch the tide and yet locked into a dispute with another trader. All of the men there would have known all about arbitration, how it would work and what would happen. The whole procedure would have been part of their elementary training because it would have been a day by day occurrence. It would have been the accepted custom and practice amongst the traders, they all would have known about it, probably stood around watching and waiting for the outcome, to see if the seafarer would depart on the tide with a smile upon his face or in a state of depression. But, of course, today things are more complex although the essentials are still the same. I am now absolutely convinced that the essential ingredient in arbitration, which has been absent for many a year, is that the parties understand what it is all about.

30

S... : So how shall we proceed now?

B... : Well, as I said, the law only requires consent by the parties and no more. So, apart from the sentiment that knowledge of arbitration is essential and our urging that the sentiment is passed on as a clarion call to all and sundry, I just do not know.

31 **A...** : So, we're left with greater understanding about what should be done, but no effective way of doing anything about it; other than teach everyone in the nation, or the world for that matter.

C... : That's an impossible task.

32 **B...** : Agreed. It will be an equally impossible task to change the law related to arbitration. The law on arbitration has been fundamentally static since 1889, except for the supplementary statutory amendments, most of which, it seems, have fostered a desire to seek more change rather than settle the issues. The Arbitration Act 1979, is thought by some to have been nothing other than a trigger for debate rather than a valuable piece of statute law which actually improved arbitration procedure. For example . . . .

33

S... : We must not deviate from our instant purpose. Has there been any change in the law in respect of the parties entering into an arbitration agreement of recent times?

34 **B...** : The 1889 Arbitration Act made it clear that a written agreement to submit present or future differences to arbitration was all that was necessary in order to effect arbitration within the scope of the statutes. That remains the same today. The Arbitration Act 1950 states, and I quote, ". . . the expression "*arbitration agreement*" means a written agreement to submit present or future differences to arbitration, whether an arbitrator is named therein or not."

35 **S...** : All that is necessary is a simple written agreement.

36 **B...** : Yes. There are, of course, certain qualifications to that. For example, there must be a dispute before an arbitration can be commenced. But, for practical purposes, all that is required is a simple written agreement to resolve disputes by arbitration. The parties to that agreement - no one else - are then bound to refer the matter to arbitration at the instigation of either party. Knowledge of arbitration is not an issue. Everyone within the jurisdiction is deemed to know the law and that's that.

S... : Then, I agree. There is a real problem.

A... : As our friend **B...** said, the problem seems insurmountable.

S... : It would be foolish to believe that one could resolve the issue by generally educating everyone who is likely to be in dispute. Further, it would be equally foolish to believe that one could prevent people signing an arbitration agreement prior to knowing what arbitration was all about. And, **B...** tells us that the chance of changing the law is remote. . . . Let us tackle the problem from another angle.

B... : What other angle could there be?

S... : The most important angle of all. The law cannot be changed easily. And we cannot hope to educate the masses. But we do know what triggers off arbitration, namely: the written arbitration agreement. That is the point where we can make our influence felt. Now, **B...**, my good friend, can you answer this: If people generally do not know about arbitration why would they draft an arbitration agreement?

B... : They wouldn't.

S... : Then who would?

37 **B...** : The various professional and trade bodies who prepare standard forms of contracts and those in the legal profession who incorporate arbitration agreements into special, ad hoc, contracts.

S... : Are you sure that people generally would never include an arbitration agreement of their own volition?

C... : The answer to that is obvious. If people generally do not know about arbitration or about the Arbitration Acts, how would they ever know the method of commencing an arbitration. I cannot imagine anyone sitting down with pen and paper, saying to themselves, "I must draft an arbitration agreement just in case we are in dispute with each other."

38 **A...** : I think that must be the case generally, but some bodies like the Chartered Institute of Arbitrators tell people how good arbitration is and suggest the type of agreement that should be signed.

S... : Does that Institute give any warning with such a recommendation?

39 **A...** : No. . . . Because it believes that arbitration is a good procedure for the resolution of disputes. The main objective of the Institute is that it shall promote arbitration for the resolution of disputes.

S... : So we can be fairly certain that people generally would never create an arbitration agreement, unless they happened to see the recommendation of the Chartered Institute of Arbitrators. That is very useful to know because our task will be much easier. **B...**, tell me this: If a member of the legal profession were to include an arbitration agreement within the terms of an ad hoc contract, would it be done without first telling the parties all about arbitration?

B... : I should certainly hope not. I would consider it to be an act of . . . yes, I will say it . . . an act of negligence for a member of the legal profession to include an arbitration agreement without first discussing the full implications with the client. And, presumably, the other party, or parties, to the contract will have the benefit of legal advice also.

S... : Thus, where there is an arbitration agreement within an ad hoc contract we can assume that the parties are aware of all the implications and will know sufficient about the procedure. . . . So, we would be satisfied that our criteria had been met.

B... : I would say that was the case. Or, alternatively, if it were not the case, the parties may well have recourse against their respective legal advisers for damages. Having said that, there is always the possibility, taking into account the attitude of our judges at the present time, that a judge will say that the solicitor gave the best advice even though he did not adequately inform the client.

S... : So. . . . Should we ask the professional bodies representing the lawyers to issues a statement which recommends this: That lawyers make certain that their clients understand the full implication of arbitration and also that advice be given about procedure whenever their members intend to include an arbitration agreement in any ad hoc contract? Wouldn't that remove one area of difficulty?

40 **B...** : Indeed it would. I cannot think of anything simpler. In fact, I would hope that lawyers do that already and so they would welcome the recommendation rather than oppose it. Yes, I agree, that would remove one area of difficulty. But, what about all the other standard forms of contract prepared by the professional bodies and the trade bodies?

S... : It may well be the case that we could encourage these bodies to have a two-stage agreement.

A... : Why not deal with the situation in the same way as the ad hoc contracts, namely: recommend that a warning be given?

C... : If people do not read the contracts to see that an arbitration agreement exists, or do not understand about arbitration, how can anyone be certain that a warning would be read, understood if read, or even heeded if understood?

41 **B...** : It is even more complex, in so far that some people never actually see a standard form of contract, never even know much about it, yet they refer to them in their own written contracts by incorporating the terms of the standard form with a simple reference that it be so.

42 **S...** : So, it is quite clear that the point of action must be aimed at the professional and trade bodies. I will now return to the concept of a two-stage agreement. For example, once a dispute has arisen and the parties call upon an arbitrator to resolve their differences, there could be a stage where the appointed arbitrator is bound to explain to the parties about arbitration, and also about how the dispute will be dealt with and to outline the more pertinent points which will affect the parties. If the parties then wished to proceed with arbitration - and here I refer to the "Diplock" concept of mutual obligations - then so be it. Because they will proceed with knowledge and understanding.

A... : But that may expose the arbitrator to a risk of giving negligent advice and make him liable to the parties.

B... : Moreover, one of the parties may decide not to proceed with the arbitration, and thus leave the whole thing in a complete mess.

C... : That should please the lawyers.

43 **S...** : Ignoring **C...**'s remark. And not wishing to break out into the business of judicial immunity and negligence at this stage . . . .

P... : We've completely missed coffee this morning and now lunch is on the table. We better stop now. Sorry to interrupt but we must eat.

[AFTER LUNCH]

P... : That's better, there's nothing quite like a good lunch, please continue gentlemen. We paused at the point of objections to the arbitrator giving advice and about delays.

44 **S...** : I believe the objections could be overcome. Assuming there is a break, then the arbitrator could either tell the parties about procedure or say to the parties something like this: "You now have an opportunity to seek advice about arbitrations and about the procedure before I issue my first Orders two weeks hence. Once I have issued the first Order, you will be bound by the procedure."

B... : But that would never do. In some shipping arbitrations, the arbitration commences and is completed with an award, all within a few days, let alone weeks. No. that would never do.

S... : It would not be necessary for the parties themselves to delay the proceedings. They could simply say that they knew all about the procedure and ask to get on with the business of the arbitration straightaway.

B... : Unfortunately, there will always be the party who does not want to proceed and who will create a delay even though they know all there is to know about arbitration.

45 **C...** : It is my experience that parties who wish to cause a delay never have any difficulty in any event . . . if that is what they choose to do. I personally would not concern myself about that aspect . . . providing it was considered that having such a pause would help those people who genuinely did not know about arbitration. The advantage of the latter would outweigh the former by a mile. In any event, there is no break provision at present and everyone knows about the delays that exist and, moreover, most parties in shipping disputes are represented by lawyers and they would not wish to be heard saying that their client wanted a delay to familiarise himself with arbitration procedure. Everyone would know such a request would be a sham. The lawyer calling for the delay would be rubbished by his colleagues, and rightly so. In any event, it would be a very poor lawyer who could not think up a better excuse for seeking a delay. I could, and I'm no lawyer.

S... : Then, we can assume that such a pause would not be a real hindrance in the shipping world because, for practical purposes, "the pause" would be simply technical, because the parties would invariably not seek a delay on that count.

B... : Well, all right. Let's say that there is a pause. Then, let us say that one or both parties decide that they do not want arbitration, what then?

46 **S...** : If both parties decide that they do not want arbitration after the procedure has been explained to them, it seems to me . . . as **C...** said before . . . the only potential losers will be the arbitrator and any experts involved; because they will lose their potential fees. But the parties will have saved themselves from doing something which, had they known more details earlier, they would never have ventured into in the first place and that must be good.

A... : I agree, even though I would be the loser. There is no satisfaction in being an arbitrator and realising after the event that it was not really what the parties wanted.

B... : I cannot disagree, but how would they resolve their dispute? They could not come back to arbitration twice.

A... : Why couldn't they come back twice, providing an award had not been issued.

B... : I suppose that must be the case.

S... : They would be able to resolve their dispute in a number of ways: for example, by agreement on their own, by some form of conciliation or mediation, etcetera. But, in any event, the parties are able to agree to anything they choose, so it would be up to them. All that would be different
47 would be a choice from knowledge as opposed to action in ignorance.

48 **A...** : I can tell of many occasions when I have been able to help parties in that very way. Although there was no officially agreed pause, when the parties - often unrepresented - came before me in the first instance, I have explained all about the likely procedure, costs, etcetera and after that, they have gone away and settled their dispute. However, where the parties have seemed as though they knew what they were doing I have left the running up to them. Often, when it's too late, I'm afraid to say, one discovers that they knew very little. The same is sometimes the case even when the parties have been represented by solicitors.

B... : That is all very well, but what if one party wants to proceed with the arbitration and the other party does not. Assume that . . . after someone has explained all about the procedure, etcetera . . . one of the parties is keen to proceed but the other does not wish to go ahead. That is the big stumbling block.

S... : I agree. That is the situation which must be tackled. There are two broad issues that arise: (a) a party who genuinely did not understand arbitration and after discovering all about it does not want to proceed; and (b) a party who knows all about arbitration already but who seeks only to obstruct the proceedings and prevent the other party pursuing a claim. Can you think of any other options?

B... : What you have stated will do for the present, but there are bound to be variations in the spectrum between the extremes.

49 **A...** : In a way, option (a) has already been recognised in respect of consumer disputes and there is an Act which allows the consumer to opt out. I'm not sure of the full details as I rarely deal with consumer disputes.

B... : **A...** is referring to the Consumer Arbitration Agreements Act 1988. Its purpose is to prevent an arbitration agreement being enforced against a consumer. Typically, there may be a standard form of contract for a holiday or for removal of furniture, etcetera, where the terms include an arbitration agreement binding the parties to arbitration. Under these circumstances it would not be easy for the consumer to trade outside the standard terms if all traders used them. Many complaints about the injustice of it all brought about the Act. Consumers were often faced with high-cost arbitrations to recover fairly low sums, which sums could be more easily recovered at low cost in the County Courts. And also many consumers who were entitled to legal aid would not have that benefit in arbitration. However, the Act is not based on prior knowledge about arbitration for its effect. It may well be the case that the consumer is an expert on arbitration, but wishes not to be bound by the arbitration agreement, instead preferring to deal with the matter in the County Court where comparatively risk free arbitration can be pursued.

S... : That Act seems interesting on several counts, not least by the fact that it does not seem to be too difficult to get the law changed when there is a substantial amount of complaint and a good need. . . . I do not believe anyone should be forced into a private procedure for the resolution of a dispute without being very clear about the procedure or consequences or even just be unwilling to concur in the procedure for any reason. The Act seems to be an Act for common sense.

50 **C...** : Many people in business clearly need the same protection as consumers, they are often just as vulnerable, but they do not speak with such a forceful voice. I am sure that if the Act could be extended to cover more people that would be a great help.

B... : It is easy to define a consumer, but to define "more people" is not possible.

51 **S...** :Let us deal with option (a), namely: a party who genuinely did not understand arbitration and after discovering all about it does not want to proceed. We must assume that the other party does want to proceed. We have already stated that litigation must be the default procedure in any event. So the reluctant party would need to understand that if the arbitration did not proceed and if the other party could not be persuaded to try some form of conciliation, then the only other option would be litigation. It may well be the case that when litigation is considered by the reluctant party, that arbitration may not seem so bad.

52 **A...** : I truly believe this to be the case in many disputes where the parties complain about arbitration. They complain about arbitration because they do not know what the alternatives are like. When they hear the truth about the alternatives, arbitration seems like the lesser of the evils. After all, any form

of dispute resolution is an "evil" in effect, it just happens to be a lesser evil than being in dispute.

C... : You have a good point there. I can tell you that in my opinion half of the problem lies in the fact that those who promote arbitration do not want to tell anyone about the likely problems and . . . thus . . . they just tell about the problems in other forms of dispute resolution procedures. If you spend all your time telling people to think twice before going to arbitration and tell them all about the problems, they will tell you why they need arbitration. If you keep telling people about all the benefits of arbitration, then they will tell you about all the detriments. That's human nature, isn't it?

B... : In dealing with (a), I think that you may have also dealt with (b). Because a party who knows all about arbitration already but who seeks only to obstruct the proceedings and prevent the other party pursuing a claim, may well fear litigation much more than arbitration.

S... : Thank you my good friend, you have just stolen away the affect of my next thrust. Can we think of any good reason why there should not be a break in the proceedings immediately after the appointment of the arbitrator?

A... : It is interesting that we should have reached such a conclusion. I take the silence from our friends to indicate that there is no longer any opposition to the resolution. Some years ago, I read a booklet which gave the results of a survey into arbitration procedures and made a range of recommendations. I brought the booklet along with me today. One of the recommendations was this: Under the heading: "ARBITRATION FOUND NOT SUITABLE" it read, "That an arbitrator should have a statutory right after the appointment and after the preliminary hearing to decide that, because of the circumstances of the dispute, arbitration is not suitable and that the matter is better heard by a court - subject only to the right of the parties to reaffirm jointly the arbitration agreement and appointment and to proceed with the dispute and forgoing all rights of appeal to the court, save only for serious
53 misconduct on the part of the arbitrator." . . . At the time of reading it, I considered it to be a most odd suggestion, although the concept was supported by those who responded to the survey. After the discussions which we have held, I've had a change of heart. It seems that there is a strong case for there to be a pause for reflection after the appointment of the arbitrator.

B... : There is no doubt that many arbitrations proceed in a very difficult way . . . all because of some inherent problems which cannot be corrected once the procedure has started. It is quite often the case that the full import of the matters in dispute are not realised until after the arbitration has been commenced. . . . Sometimes the parties discover that the arbitrator is not the right man for the job and then they still have to soldier on because no one wants to lose face, especially the arbitrator. Yes, on reflection, I could now go on all day promoting the cause for there to be a break for reflection, be it explanation about arbitration and litigation or for other sound reasons.

C... : Then let's get on with passing our thoughts to the professional and trade bodies who draft these arbitration agreements so that they can do something constructive about it. But I believe it will be difficult to convince them . . . . The big point about our discussions is recognising a need for there to be a time for reflection by the parties. . . . So that the most appropriate forum can be selected. A simple option for arbitration decided at the time of
54 signing a contract is the last choice, once taken.

55 **S...** : So what we have concluded is this: That in all arbitration agreements there would be much benefit, and no significant detriment, for there to be a pause in the proceedings immediately after the appointment of the arbitrator so that the parties can reflect upon the significance of the step which they have taken. And, in particular, that this step should be taken to ensure that the parties are made fully aware of all the factors attendant upon resolving a dispute by arbitration. Furthermore, that such a provision should be preferably incorporated into an Arbitration Act or, alternatively, provided for in the arbitration agreements incorporated within standard forms of contract.

P... : This may well be a good time to pause for the day.

S... : An excellent suggestion.

[10.00 a.m. DAY 3 OF DISCUSSION]

P... : Well, gentlemen, having reached a conclusion last night, we can enter upon another topic.

S... : The conclusion reached last night was a mere step on the way towards understanding. We had started off by seeking to understand the nature of the agreement between the parties and their relationship. The stage reached was simply part of that agreement, simply stating that the parties ought to be provided with a definite break point following the appointment of an arbitrator so that it could be established that they knew about the procedure which they had selected. What we need to establish is this: When the parties enter into an agreement to resolve their differences by arbitration, what is
56 the nature of that agreement, what is their true relationship?

B... : We need spend but little time on that. The relationship is simply a contractual one, nothing more, nothing less.

S... : So, let us assume that the parties have adopted a simple agreement which states, "The undersigned hereby agree that all differences between them shall be settled by arbitration." Is that sufficient?

B... : Yes, absolutely.

S... : What would happen if there were a breach of that contract?

B... : A breach of a contract to refer a matter to arbitration? . . . That's not possible.

S... : I had understood that if any party entered into a contract and failed to abide by the terms, then that would be a breach, which would give rise to damages. If the agreement to arbitrate is a contract between two or more parties, what happens if it is not possible to breach the contract?

B... : Well, the fact is this, an agreement to arbitrate is not like a contract to undertake some task, it is an agreement to be bound by a certain procedure to settle differences between the parties.

S... : And, if one of the parties does not abide by that procedure, will he be in breach of contract and will he be liable to damages?

B... : No. Not in the sense that you speak of. But he may suffer some penalty.

57 **S...** : I did not think that it was possible in a private contract for one party to have power to impose a penalty upon the other for a breach.

58 **B...** : Well perhaps I used the word penalty in the wrong sense. One party wouldn't have power to impose a penalty upon the other, but the arbitrator would, no doubt penalise, in some way, the offending party.

S... : As in the form of fine?

B... : No. No. Of course not. An arbitrator does not have any power to impose a fine in anyway whatsoever.

S... : Then . . . as in the form of depriving one party of some entitlement?

B... : Well, not that either. Perhaps more in the form of allocating costs unfavourably against the offending party.

S... : Surely that would amount to a penalty or a fine.

B... : No. Not if is was justified.

S... : How do you define justified?

B... : I would say that where a party deserved to be. . . . Well, say. . . . It's very difficult to put it in a way that would suit you. . . . because it is a discretion which would be within the power of the arbitrator to do what he believed was right and proper.

S... : Subjectively or objectively?

B... : Certainly not subjectively. Cost must be allocated according to principles set down by precedent based on decisions of the courts.

S... : How then, would the arbitrator be able to levy costs in a way that would be unfavourable against the offending party?

59 **B...** : Put like that, the arbitrator would not have a power to penalise. He would only have power to allocate the costs based on established principles. Which principles may well mean that the offending party will occur a greater burden of costs as a result of his . . . his . . . .

S... : Let me put an example forward. Two people are in dispute and they have a written agreement to resolve their disputes by arbitration. One party has built a brick wall for the other and wants to be paid £1,000. A price was not previously agreed and the other party does not wish to pay more than £500. The other party is quite aware of the agreement to resolve disputes by arbitration, but he just ignores the whole thing and refuses to do anything or take part in any way, but he does tender the £500, which is refused. The first party seeks the appointment of an arbitrator and accordingly one is appointed. What then?

A... : I have dealt with several such cases, so I can speak from experience. Briefly, I would try to get both parties to take part in the arbitration but, in any event, I would never do anything about which both parties were not fully aware. Assuming that the party, said to be owing the money, takes no part whatsoever, I would order the claimant to make his claim, which would be served on the respondent, who would be asked to make a reply, or to use the right term, serve a defence. In our example, nothing would happen. . . . I would then give at least three further orders for the respondent to comply and serve his defence. If all other things were straightforward, I would then
60 proceed ex parte towards a final award.

S... : Tell us how you would do that.

61 **A...** : Being an expert in the field of the dispute, I would have the benefit of knowing the subject matter in some detail; and I would have already advised both parties of my expertise. So proceeding ex parte, I would ask the
62 claimant to prove his case. It is always up to the claimant to prove his case on the balance of probability. If the claimant satisfied me that £1,000 was the correct sum, I would make an award accordingly. And by virtue of my powers, derived from the arbitration agreement, I would order that therespondent pay the costs of the arbitration; because the claimant had been successful. The claimant . . . then . . . could recover the £1,000 plus the costs from the respondent. And, if the respondent did not pay, the award could be registered as judgment of the court.

63

S... : But you would not have awarded £1,000 unless you were quite satisfied that it was the proper sum, would you?

A... : No.

S... : So, even if the respondent had taken a full part in the arbitration, in the particular example used, you would still have awarded £1,000 plus costs against the respondent.

A... : Of course.

S... : What would have been the situation, if the respondent took no part, and yet the claimant failed to persuade you that the wall was worth any more than £500?

A... : I would say that the claimant had failed to prove his case and would state that in my award, which award would order the claimant to pay the costs of the arbitration.

S... : That is most interesting. Because it seems to me from what you say that the respondent would have taken the correct course of action by staying away.

A... : How so?

S... : If he fulfilled his part in the arbitration, he would be bound to incur some direct cost in doing so, as well as the costs which you had awarded in any event. So, taking the first case, the respondent would have to pay the £1,000 plus costs in your award for your own fees and costs of the claimant together with his own costs. Furthermore, the costs would have no doubt been higher because, by him attending, more time would have been spent in exchange of papers and argument, that is for certain. Taking the second case, the claimant would still have lost, even though the respondent had taken a full part in the arbitration, but in addition the claimant would have had to pay the respondent's costs for taking part in the arbitration.

A... : I follow your reasoning, but the hypothetical case was merely chosen to serve your point.

S... : That's the point of hypothetical cases.

A... : But most cases are more complex and if the respondent does not take part the arbitrator may be persuaded on points which might have been successfully challenged by the respondent; who would then suffer the consequences.

64 S... : The difference between us is this: I am trying to establish a principle about the basis of the arbitration agreement and whether or not one party can be penalised for breach of contract. Whereas, you are trying to envisage what may happen when the respondent fails to successfully counter the proof of the claimant. Which situation, with due respect, may be exactly the same whether the respondent had turned up or not. In fact, it must sometimes be the case that when a respondent stands before you that he is more help in assisting you to find for the claimant than the claimant himself.

A... : I understand what you say, but I fail to see the point of it.

S... : Simply this: in the example given, the respondent actually benefited from his breach, or his total failure to take part in the arbitration, so there
65 cannot be an absolute concept of breach of an agreement in the normally accepted contractual sense. So, the agreement to go to arbitration cannot be a simple contract in the sense that one normally accepts.

B... : I need to think about that. I agree that there is not a direct relationship between allocation of costs and . . . well, say a breach . . . of the arbitration agreement, but one cannot move too far away from the duty of each party to comply with the agreement.

S... : Well, perhaps you will explain what compliance with the agreement means, what are all the express terms with which the parties must comply and what is the burden to be suffered by a failure to comply?

B... : In our example of an arbitration agreement, there is only one express term, namely: to settle any difference by arbitration. And, we have just analysed one aspect where failure to comply did not lead directly to any burden being suffered for the failure.

S... : Then, what are the implied terms that must be complied with?

66 **B...** : That's not an easy question to answer. Some of them will be found in the Arbitration Acts, some in any supplementary actions which the parties may take, some in the inherent powers of an arbitrator gained by custom and by virtue of case law.

S... : So my dear **B...**, what you are telling us is than an arbitration agreement - whatever it may be - is an exceedingly complex thing to understand.

B... : I'm afraid so.

S... : Do you believe anyone really understands it?

67 **B...** : I doubt it. No, not in any absolute sense.

S... : Not in the remote sense either. It is surely the case, as reflected from our own progress in trying to understand these basic points, that there is much to be settled before one can understand the true meaning and effect of an arbitration agreement.

B... : I believe that I could answer more positively on some of these issues, following some detailed research.

S... : You are an experienced lawyer in the field of arbitration, so what
68 chance do the parties to an arbitration agreement have. They, presumably,
are simply expected to put their faith in a system and the experts who
operate within it. A most unsatisfactory state of affairs I would say. I'm
absolutely convinced that our idea that there should be an agreed pause after
the appointment of an arbitrator is essential for the benefit of the parties and
for the procedure as a whole.

B... : I see that coffee has arrived, I could just do with a cup.

P... : An excellent idea.

[POST COFFEE]

69 **S...** : **B...** told us over coffee that every simple contract depends on
consideration for its effect, so it may be helpful to investigate the
consideration applicable to an arbitration agreement.

B... : As I said, an arbitration agreement has no effect and is of no benefit or
detriment whatsoever, unless the parties find themselves in dispute, so the
70 consideration is not like other forms of contract. I must admit that the topic
of consideration has not really been raised in the context of an arbitration
agreement as far as I am aware, but I expect some one will tell me I'm
wrong. In any event, no one has spoken to me about it before and I've not
thought about it before.

S... : That's an honest admission. But during the coffee break you did say that, "unless the arbitration is in the form of a deed, then there must be some form of consideration otherwise the agreement to arbitrate would not be enforceable."

C... : I'm no lawyer, but surely, consideration is irrelevant. Surely the force of
the agreement derives all its power from s. 32 of the Arbitration Act 1950. If
the parties sign a written agreement that comes within the provisions of s. 32,
71 then that is an arbitration agreement by definition and, accordingly, has all
the force necessary to bring into play the case law and statute law related to
arbitration. And, the parties are bound accordingly.

B... : Where did you read that?

C... : I didn't. It just seems to be simple logic. Otherwise how would the agreement work. As you said, "an arbitration agreement has no effect and is of no benefit or detriment whatsoever, unless the parties find themselves in dispute." No one knows, at the time of entering into the agreement, which party may call upon the power vested in the agreement, nor under what circumstances, unless of course a dispute has arisen first.

B... : In some ways, I believe you may have touched upon a useful explanation. I must say that I feel rather lost because, reluctant as I am to admit to it, I have never given the topic much thought. Lawyers, of my time, never had any basic training in arbitration. Most of us picked up our personal knowledge from private study, usually learnt "on the hoof" as one undertakes the case for a client.

C... : That's what we call learning by experience, at the client's expense.

A... : What other way is there, if the truth were known?

S... : Let us not deviate. Can we conclude that consideration is not a factor in terms of an agreement to arbitrate?

72 **B...** : No. . . . I just cannot accept that consideration is not present; that would go against all my training and experience. I think consideration must be present in the concept that both parties agree not to settle disputes by litigation. I'm sure that must be the consideration.

S... : That would seem to be an inherent part of the agreement, it would be the purpose of the agreement. If the whole purpose of the agreement is to ensure arbitration instead of litigation, how can that be the consideration for entering into the agreement?

B... : Well, that's it, isn't it? The total agreement is nothing other than the consideration itself. Yes . . . I believe that is the very point. An arbitration
73 agreement is simply an expression of consideration by the parties not to do one thing, namely; not to litigate. It does not prevent them from unilaterally attempting to negotiate, from conciliating, from mediating, nor from anything else other than litigation. And, the consideration in return for not going to litigation is an agreement to seek arbitration as opposed to litigation as the default procedure for resolving any dispute. I'm sure that must be right. But, equally I have some doubts because I have always accepted that the agreement was a contract in the ordinary sense and I have never thought any more about it. I may wish to come back on this topic.

S... : By all means let us review the topic. We do not have the power to write things down in tablets of stone to endure for all time. We are simply trying to understand what is already there. If it's subsequently shown that our understanding is wrong, we must be the first to change our views on the matter.

A... : The power of the contract as we generally understand it cannot be really present. For example, if there were a dispute about the agreement to arbitrate and one party decided to go to litigation instead. What then?

B... : That is fairly simple to answer, because the court would simply enforce the arbitration agreement.

C... : They may at the present time, but that was not always the case.

B... : I was speaking in general terms. A judge of the court today would usually stay the litigation pending arbitration. Nevertheless, the court does have a discretion in the matter.

74 **S...** : So the parties are not in total control of the arbitration procedure. The arbitration agreement can be overridden by the court.

B... : Yes, but it would be most unusual.

S... : But is it a possibility?

B... : Yes.

S... : Could the court overrule the terms of a normal contract in any circumstances?

B... : That is a very big question, but generally, no. The courts would enforce the terms of a contract, unless there was some question of public policy, or of some specific statute that made the contract or some of its terms illegal or unenforceable.

S... : So an arbitration agreement is significantly different from a normal contract in that respect as well.

A... : A judge cannot prevent arbitration, just because he does not agree with the procedure or the agreement.

B... : I believe that it should be put the other way round, namely: That a judge can prevent a party taking a dispute to litigation if he is satisfied that the matter in dispute can be dealt with properly by arbitration and also if he is satisfied that a valid arbitration agreement is in existence.

S... : All these things point towards the conclusion that we have been reaching about the nature of the agreement to arbitrate.

75 **B...** : It may be useful to look at s. 4(1) of the Arbitration Act 1950. That section gives the court the power to stay legal proceedings if it is satisfied that there is no sufficient reason why the matter should not be referred to arbitration in accordance with the arbitration agreement.

C... : Presumably the expression, "legal proceedings" means the same as litigation. After all, arbitration is not an illegal proceeding, is it?

B... : I think that we can safely assume that the section means litigation.

S... : So, the court has a wide discretion without any real qualification.

B... : Yes, it will decide each case upon its merits.

S... : Then the attempts of the parties to avoid litigation may well be frustrated, thus indicating that their agreement to do something is definitely not the final word as between them. Clearly the court maintains wide powers although, as you say, it will only exercise them when it sees a real need to do so.

B... : Yes. Generally speaking, providing the applicant to the court confirms his willingness to go to arbitration then the matter will be stayed in most ordinary cases.

S... : Is the confirmation of the applicant's willingness to go to arbitration just part of the process of persuading the judge to exercise his discretion in favour of the applicant?

76 **B...** : No. That is an express part of s. 4(1).

S... : Please read out that part.

B... : I'll start from "sufficient reason." It reads, ". . . if satisfied that there is no sufficient reason why the matter should not be referred [to arbitration] in accordance with the [arbitration] agreement, and the applicant was, at the time when the proceedings [litigation] were commenced, and still remains, ready and willing to do all things necessary to the proper conduct of the arbitration, [the court or a judge thereof] may make an order staying the proceedings."

S... : How very interesting.

B... : In what way?

77 **S...** : You will recall that you spoke about Lord Diplock and his concept of mutual obligations of the parties in arbitration?

B... : Yes.

S... : Can you see that the section which you have just read to us, is simply a confirmation of the principle of mutual obligation? The court would not allow an arbitration to proceed without the restatement of the original commitment to be ready and willing to proceed with the arbitration and do all the things necessary for its proper conduct. That commitment is being
78 sought from the respondent, who would normally be the applicant, that is, the one who is seeking to prevent the claimant pursuing the matter through the courts.

P... : We must break for lunch now.

[POST LUNCH]

S... : Having listened carefully to the cross-table banter and discussions over lunch, I would like you all to consider the concept that the arrangement
79 between the parties is simply a fiduciary one.

B... : Fiduciary. Well, I would accept that many aspects of any arrangement could have a fiduciary element and I would not gainsay that an arbitration agreement had a fiduciary element, but to say that it was simply a fiduciary arrangement. . . . Well . . . that must go too far.

S... : A fiduciary arrangement is the only concept that goes far enough to cover the agreement. The standard concepts are: Trustee-Beneficiary; Director-Company; Agent-Principal; Partner-Partner; Solicitor-Client; Doctor-Patient; Parent-Child; etcetera. So why not Party-Party in arbitration. Most Fiduciary relationships arise out of some form of agreement in the first place, but the fiduciary element transcends the simple concepts of that agreement.

A... : I don't know where this is taking us.

C... : Nor do I. Does it even matter, in any event?

S... : If I were to state it this way: That there is no consideration in an arbitration agreement except one: namely, not to proceed with litigation in order that the dispute may be resolved by arbitration as the final default
80 procedure. And, that the arbitration agreement creates a fiduciary relationship to be ready and willing to do all things necessary for the proper conduct of the arbitration; whichever of the parties may seek to activate the agreement at the time of a dispute. Further, that there are no direct penalties for any party failing to honour the agreement; there are only the consequences of neglect to do what is necessary to bring about an award.

B... : I would need to think about that very carefully.

S... : Of course, I understand that each and every word in such a statement would need to be carefully considered but, following on from all our discussions, are you able to accept the concept generally?

B... : Subject to some further thought on the subject, I can see the force in the argument. It is quite clear that the simple concepts which I have always held about the agreement being just a contractual one have been torn off their moorings. Something has to replace that and perhaps that something will take the form which you have stated.

C... : **B...** is waffling, so I think he means, yes.

B... : This matter goes to the root of arbitration and we must not accept anything without testing the concepts over a wider body of opinion.

81 **S...** : I agree, that must be the case, whether we were to seek it or not. I am all in favour for having these conclusions tested in wider public debate.

A... : I readily admit to my failing to see the point of the conclusion, so perhaps wider debate will help me understand why it is necessary to analyse the relationship.

P... : I can see that a significant moment has been reached. If nothing else, I can see that all present have given the best of their own thoughts to the subject. I have made a note of all that which has been stated . . . a little editing here or there, maybe . . . so that others can consider the arguments. We must wait and see whether they are rejected or accepted. I think we may conclude the day here and start an entirely new topic for day-four of our discussion.

S... : My dear **P...**, I am sure that you have fairly represented the didactical efforts of all here, so I believe it must stand as it is, without any editing whatsoever. Otherwise, we shall all desire to remove the worst of our arguments and statements, leaving only that which we believe to be sensible and good. Any reader, without seeing all our observations . . . good or bad . . . which have led to conclusions, might just as well be given only the conclusions set down in a simple statement. But, I suspect, they would have to travel the same ground that we have spent so much time going over. No, please leave all of it as it is. We must each suffer the humiliation arising from our ill-thought-out comments as well as any recognition for those comments which have lasting value.

A... : I reluctantly agree to what you have said. But before we close our discussion, I would like to say that the fiduciary element is a concept that I have never understood. If the agreement is to be identified as setting up a fiduciary relationship, does that mean that all the other obligations which may have been incorporated into an arbitration agreement are of no consequence?

B... : No. . . . Fiduciary is a word which is used so freely and loosely by the legal profession that it often causes confusion to others. But it is not wrong to use the word in that way. The word simply means "Trust" and I do not know of many relationships at all that could survive without an element of trust. It does not depend upon any particular circumstance and it exists in almost
82 every concept that one can imagine. An old judgment identified "fiduciary" as being necessary for the preservation of mankind; and I suppose that must be about the widest concept of trust that one could have. Where express terms set out the relative position of the parties to any arrangement, then the fiduciary element must, in similar proportion, be squeezed out of the arrangement, but I do not believe that it can ever be squeezed out altogether, no matter how hard the parties may try. I suppose that I would say that historically the development of the law of equity was the simple recognition of the existence of the fiduciary element in any arrangement. Now, it is quite clear that in a fiduciary relationship there is an understanding that one party owes a duty of care to the other party, which duty transcends any written agreement; except, of course, where the written agreement specifically excludes the particular duty of care. There is a duty of care, for example, not to profit at the expense of the other party, except as specifically provided for by the express terms of the contract. As a general example of a simple
83 concept, the law is this: that all parties have a duty to mitigate the effect of any damages which they may suffer as a result of a breach of contract, or

indeed, likewise any damages arising under the law of tort. Put simply, the
global word for all these things is the word "Fiduciary." Of course, the word
is not used to identify express concepts of law, the like of which I have just
mentioned. Rather, it provides the broad concept for implied concepts of
law; i.e., when suffering from a breach the party suffering has a duty to
ensure that he does not profit by the breach nor does he make the party
responsible for the breach suffer any detriment beyond that which is just. . . .
I feel that I am rambling on at the close of the day, but what I was leading up
to is this: That a party in arbitration owes a duty of care to the other party to
ensure that the dispute between them is resolved without seeking to profit
from the manipulation of the procedure, likewise without seeking to make
84 the other party suffer. This was, I now believe, the "Diplock" concept of
85 mutual obligation, this is the concept of s. 4(1) of the Arbitration Act 1950,
86 and also s. 12 of the same Act. For arbitration to work effectively, the parties
should seek only to resolve their dispute in a just manner. They should not
seek to cause the procedure to be part of the means for self-profit or a
detriment to the other side. Parties with such intentions should be denied the
right . . . nay, I would say privilege . . . to private arbitration and be left to
face the full force of litigation. It is always the genuine party who will suffer
87 from a recalcitrant and devious party in private arbitration, it is a fallacy to
believe otherwise. So, it is never in the interest of a genuine party to agree for
future disputes to be locked into arbitration. . . . However, to deal with the
point about express terms in an arbitration agreement I can say this: That the
parties can expressly agree anything which they wish, and it is often wise to
do so. They may include agreements about the type of arbitrator, the type of
procedure, the extent of the arbitrator's powers, the make-up of the tribunal,
and the like things. But, if they agree . . . prior to a dispute arising . . . that
there shall be no legal representation or that each party shall bear its own
88 costs in a future dispute, then, the law will override such agreements.
And . . . .

S... : I am sorry to stop you at this point, my dear **B....** But I think you have got
the wind in your sails and you may go on for a long time. You seemed to have
found the conviction of a convert, and I'm pleased. . . . To have moved the
thinking of a lawyer on such an issue, is the first step to converting the
89 masses, or at least those who are able to effect change as opposed to those
who simply speak about it.

90 **C...** : That's a very profound statement. You only have to see how lawyers have jumped onto the band-wagon of ADR to find your proof.

A... : It's not just lawyers. It seems that everyone is being carried forward on the tide of ADR.

S... : Perhaps that's because arbitration is floundering on the high-seas. Let's hope that **B...**'s new found vigour will help to settle arbitration once again as the true alternative default procedure for the resolution of disputes; within, of course, the framework of the ultimate default procedure: litigation. No ADR procedure, bar arbitration, can ever claim that position; and none ever could.

B... : I don't admit to being convinced, I was just going over the issues.

[10.00 a.m. DAY-4 OF DISCUSSION]

S... : I believe we can assume that our thoughts about the relationship of the parties have been exhausted. What is to be the next topic?

91 **A...** : We ought to proceed with the relationship between the parties and the arbitrator, then we can proceed on to the business of judicial immunity and the terms of engagement.

B... : With due respect, the terms of engagement are one and the same as the relationship.

A... : I do understand that. What I really meant was this: How can we sort out the terms of engagement at the time of the appointment?

S... : It seems a logical step, so let's do that.

THE AGREEMENT BETWEEN THE ARBITRATOR AND THE PARTIES

S... : Let us ask **B...** to put us right on the current law.

B... : After our previous discussions over the last few days, I would say that your request is more akin to leading me into exposing my lack of knowledge rather than a desire for your edification.

S... : I believe that progress will be best served by my saying nothing. Please, my dear **B...**, at least lead us into the topic.

B... : Having discussed relationships over the last few days, I would be quite satisfied by saying this: That if the relationship between the parties was one of a fiduciary relationship brought into being by an agreement between the parties, then the same is more than appropriate for the relationship between
92 the parties and the arbitrator. We know that the arbitration does not commence until an arbitrator accepts the appointment, so that acceptance concludes the agreement, and that agreement brings into play the fiduciary relationship.

C... : Is that correct?

A... : It is, as far as I'm concerned. Until I accept an appointment, there is no appointment and thus no arbitration.

C... : I thought that the arbitration commenced upon the notice of one party to the other.

93 **B...** : Yes, that is correct. Section 29 of the Arbitration Act 1950, sets down the point at which an arbitration is commenced. But we are discussing the relationship between the arbitrator and the parties, and that does not commence until acceptance of the appointment by the chosen arbitrator; which acceptance may occur before a dispute has arisen, e.g., if the arbitrator has agreed to be named in an arbitration agreement prior to a dispute arising. Sometimes, of course, where the arbitrator has not been selected, even though the arbitration has commenced, it may be years before an arbitrator is appointed and accepts the appointment. This may happen when there are procedural disputes, or disputes about whether the arbitrator should be a certain type of person, the possibilities are endless.

C... : It is always possible to make an application to the court for an appointment. . . . If there are likely to be such problems, although I must say that I have never experienced too much delay in getting an arbitrator appointed. . . . I wonder how that would affect our suggestion of a pause for
94 reflection by the parties after the appointment of an arbitrator.

95 **B...** : That is a difficult point to answer. But, if there were undue delays, I would issue a writ to commence proceedings in the court and leave it for the recalcitrant party to apply under s. 4(1) of the 1950 Act for a stay. That is bound to put pressure upon the respondent.

C... : But what if it is the claimant who is dragging his feet, what then?

96 **A...** : That would be like the problem giving rise to the mutual obligation situation; the "Diplock" concept.

S... : We must not get too side-tracked. It is only ever possible to deal with the mainstream of situations. That's why one has to always rely upon litigation as the default system. Too often, people forget that it would be impossible to legislate for everything and every situation, someone has to have the power to fill in the gaps and provide the discretionary element to all things. The real danger occurs when the default system, the final discretionary power, is clogged up with dealing with the ordinary: i.e., the
97 mainstream of cases which can be - or should be - more effectively dealt with by the procedures of arbitration, conciliation, mediation, etcetera. So please do not deviate from the main-stream of arbitrations.

B... : Then let us assume than an arbitrator has been selected.

A... : Selected by whom, the parties or an appointing body.

B... : Say, selected by an appointing body because that seems to be the usual.

C... : In several of my disputes, each side have selected their own arbitrator and the two selected arbitrators have chosen a third, the chairman.

S... : If we use the term tribunal instead of arbitrator, does it matter how the tribunal is selected providing it ends up as the tribunal?

A... : That is the big issue, because it does matter. If the tribunal, be it a sole arbitrator or several, is selected by the agreement of the parties then the parties and the tribunal can sort out the express terms for the agreement between all those involved. And, once such express terms are accepted,
98 then the tribunal is able to accept the appointment, knowing the basis of the appointment. Whereas, if the tribunal is appointed by anyone other than all the parties, how can the appointment be accepted without settling the express terms?

S... : Are we agreed upon this: That once a tribunal. . . . Let's say arbitrator for ease of reference . . . and mean sole arbitrator or any other number. . . .
99 That once a person is installed as the arbitrator, the agreement is the same in all cases, subject only to any express terms that may be incorporated.

B... : I believe that must be the case. If no express terms were incorporated, then all arbitrators, once installed, would be governed by the same implied
100 terms. For example, they would be only entitled to charge a reasonable fee, which would be subject to taxation by the courts. And, moreover, they would be bound to fulfil the duties of an arbitrator until such time as the arbitration was concluded by a final award or the agreement of the parties; or equally pertinent today the bankruptcy or liquidation of one or both parties.

S... : So what is wrong with that. If all arbitrators and all parties had the same terms, which would be implied, then all would be on a common basis and everyone would know where they stood; wouldn't they?

A... : Yes, except for this: where would I be able to find out the implied terms before acceptance of the appointment?

101 **B...** : That's a very difficult matter, because no one would ever know for certain.

S... : Why is that?

B... : Some implied terms would be found in the various statutes and statutory instruments, some would be found in the cases decided over the last few hundred years.

A... : Years ago, as a matter of interest, I added up all the cases in Mustill &
102 Boyd's book "Commercial Arbitration." I did it only for the first edition, I
did not bother any more. They quoted from nearly thirteen hundred cases,
of which well over four hundred cases were judgments between 1889 and
1950, i.e., between the two major Arbitration Acts of those dates. And, over
three hundred and fifty judgments were made before 1889.

C... : People constantly complain that case-law simply provides a field-day
103 for the lawyers. Moreover, they complain that statute law is so poorly put
together that it is impossible to determine the meaning without reference to
all the relevant case-law. Commercial men are in constant fear of what may
come up next from a judgment of the court. Over and over again principles
are being reviewed and questioned.

B... : I would say that our friend, C..., is being a bit dramatic in his view. English case law is recognised throughout the world as the most comprehensive system of any country.

C... : I don't deny that, but look at the cost to the litigants and others who
have to conform to the law within the jurisdiction. It's all very well to say
that many foreigners use our litigation system because they prefer it. But
they can come to this country, take a matter up to the House of Lords for a
104 decision, which turns our law upside down, and then go away and never use
the English legal system again.

105 B... : I must say, my dear C..., that I had never really thought about that point before. Most of my thoughts have been based on the pride of knowing that foreigners come here in preference to their own countries.

C... : Perhaps they just enjoy the experience, like foreign visitors like to witness the changing of the guards at Buckingham Palace.

B... : I doubt it very much, litigation is too expensive for simple entertainment.

106 C... : Do you really think so. It seems to me that many of the cases that have got to the House of Lords were based on relatively minor sums. I may be wrong, but that's how it seems to me.

B... : It's true that some of the House of Lords' decisions are about relatively minor sums, but that is not the point. The House of Lords' decisions are about significant points of law that set the principles for all other courts. Often, the litigants are fighting matters of principle which will have a significant effect upon the whole jurisdiction.

C... : Precisely, many foreigners come here and establish principles of law,
but they will have the choice about whether they will be bound by that law
in the future. Because on their next transaction they may choose the law of
France. When **B...** seeks to raise some doubts about the significant
fundamental changes in the law, I would just say to him this: That since
107 Lord Denning retired, many of us commercial-men have had to rethink
about the whole aspect of contracting. Take issues like fundamental breach
for example. Or, the very issue about which we are presently discussing,
namely: duty of care . . . .

S... : Hold your talk my good friends. These are very interesting matters, but they do not advance our thinking upon the topic under discussion. Except that I can see why our good friend, **A...**, is so concerned about relying upon implied terms forming the basis of the agreement between the arbitrator and the parties. With so much uncertainty, it seems to me that it is essential that there must be a point in time in any arbitration when essential terms can be expressly agreed between the arbitrator and the parties. However, the agreement of express terms does not in any way affect the concept of the fiduciary relationship that is bound to exist.

B... : I agree. Because if . . . for example . . . the parties and the arbitrator
agreed that they could totally disregard the law and just decide the matter
108 based on whatever the arbitrator thought was fair, then the courts would
not enforce the award as an arbitration award under the Arbitration Acts.

C... : What has that got to do with a fiduciary relationship?

B... : Er . . . well. . . . I'm not sure. . . . I think my mind wandered a little. . . .
I'm not used to all this cross-examination about what I say and it's
becoming a little difficult. . . . I think that what I had in mind was this: That
the fiduciary duty of the arbitrator extends beyond the relationship he has
with the parties and encompasses a wider duty to the law of the land and
the procedure of arbitration generally. . . . Yes . . . I think that's it. . . . An
109 arbitrator has a fiduciary duty to the community at large to do the job
properly and not to bring arbitration into disrepute. . . . Yes, that's it . . . he
has an overriding duty to everyone, i.e., the nation, the legal system and all
things generally.

C... : My, my. You are talking on elevated plains, aren't you?

B... : No, not really. When one realises the enormous power of an arbitrator. . . . That the power is recognised by the court when an award is enforced. . . . One has to accept that the courts are prepared to acknowledge that power because they accept that an arbitrator acts in a fiduciary way. . . . He acts with an equal duty to both the parties and also an overriding duty to society generally. . . . If that wasn't the case, then an arbitrator and the parties could enter into some kind of arrangement between themselves which would be detrimental the judicial system generally. . . . I can't think of a good example at present but, no doubt, I will.

S... : How about an arbitrator assisting the parties to put together a preliminary point of law for determination by the courts with a view to changing the law?

B... : How do you mean?

S... : Supposing both the parties and the arbitrator were in collusion with the intent of changing the law. They could set down the case in such a manner that it may influence the court to decide in the way they sought. . . . Bearing in mind that they would be seeking to change the law . . . if they failed . . . the law would simply remain the same, there would be no other backlash. . . . These wicked people would present their case before the court, making sure that all the main arguments are made in favour of the outcome which they seek. The party chosen to lose would put forward a
110 very poor case. These wicked people could then appeal up through the system hoping that one of the higher courts would favour the desired outcome. Once they had the judgment they sought, they could stop the proceedings and it would take years for anyone else to remedy the problem.

B... : But that could never happen, because the lawyers who represented them would be "Officers" of the court and duty bound not to do such a thing.

S... : Precisely, the court relies upon the fiduciary duty of lawyers towards the court. Likewise, the court relies upon the fiduciary duty of an arbitrator, because they would accept that a case put forward for determination by an arbitrator was the product of some genuine concern for the purposes of dealing properly with the arbitration.

B... : So you think that an arbitrator has the same duty to the court as a lawyer?

S... : I was simply providing an example to complete your reasoning.

A... : The duty to the court is not an odd one, because expert witnesses have an overriding duty to the court as well.

S... : Let's sum up: (a) That an arbitrator has a wider fiduciary duty than do the parties; and (b) that there needs to be some way in which essential express terms can be established prior to an arbitrator agreeing to accept
111 the appointment.

B... : And also that the relationship between the arbitrator and the parties is triggered off by an agreement . . . .

S... : Yes, of course.

112 **C...** : I believe that the point stated earlier is the relevant one, namely: That if there were no express agreement between the parties and the arbitrator, other than the simple acceptance of the appointment, then the implied terms for all installed arbitrators, sole or otherwise, would be the same in every case. Moreover, that the fiduciary element would be the most significant aspect of the agreement.

S... : I believe you have summarised the situation exactly.

C... : Right, then first: we need to know what those implied terms would be. And, secondly: what express terms would an arbitrator or the parties seek to impose to replace or supplement any of the implied terms?

B... : I agree with **C...**'s summary. But I would say that it would be almost an impossible task to identify the implied terms, beyond the obvious ones. It would be more productive to decide what the express terms should be and then to find a way of making it possible to set them down before the arbitrator is faced with having to accept the appointment.

S... : It seems logical to start off with trying to find a way of implementing express terms. If we cannot do that then the actual express terms which we would like to see could never be implemented in any event. And, of course, we can have no influence whatsoever over the implied terms . . . if we could they would not be implied terms. It seems clear to me that terms which can be implied can only ever be based on objective concepts and never the
113 product of subjective view.

C... : Unless the view of a judge is subjective when deciding what the implied terms are.

B... : Judges would never fall into the trap of being subjective . . . well, at least, not when deciding upon implied terms, so what **S...** has said is correct.

P... : I think that the coffee must be nearly cold, let's pause.

C... : A good idea.

[POST COFFEE]

S... : That was an interesting interlude . . . listening to the banter . . . over coffee . . . about whether or not . . . or whether it was simply a matter of degree . . . that subjectiveness creeps into the decisions of the court . . .
114 when in fact it shouldn't. . . . However, one cannot gainsay that implied terms should always be the product of an objective decision. . . . But let's ask **B...** to start the discussion about the implementation of express terms prior to the acceptance of an arbitrator's appointment.

B... : We must return to the similar problems which we encountered with the relationship between the parties and "the pause." I believe it is quite clear that parties who know nothing about arbitration would never knowingly enter into an arbitration agreement of their own volition, so they
115 would never be faced with the problem of implementing express terms concerning the appointment of an arbitrator. In any event . . . if they did . . . and if they approached a person to act as arbitrator, there would be an opportunity for them all to discuss the terms of the arbitrator's appointment. . . . If it so happened that neither the parties nor the arbitrator knew about arbitration . . . and that can easily happen . . . they would all be blind to the need for any form of agreement . . . at least, they would all be compatible one with the other.

C... : What you have just said is likely to have been the general case, historically speaking. People in dispute may have had a vague concept of arbitration. They may have approached a local personality who also had a vague concept only. Together, they may have gone through the motions of
116 what they believed was an arbitration procedure. . . . The arbitrator may have made a decision which the parties accepted; because they believed they would be bound; because they respected the knowledge and the authority of the arbitrator. . . . Everyone would have gone away contented that their dispute had been settled by arbitration and that was that.

117 **A...** : Never mind historically, I truly believe the same happens very much today. If we accept that the majority of parties do not know much about

arbitration, and if we accept that most arbitrators may lack complete knowledge. Then we must accept that much of what is called arbitration is in fact not arbitration.

118 **C...** : Personally, I do not believe the circumstances which you have described are necessarily a bad thing. The people involved are resolving disputes in a way that suits them. And, let's face it, one of the real problems is this: That even the "so called" experts do not necessarily know what arbitration is for certain.

B... : Dear old **C...** is again driving down the wrong lane in seeking to imply that no one really knows what arbitration is all about.

C... : Well my good friends, we are a typical example of "so called" experts . . . and we have displayed in our discussions over these last few days how difficult it is to get to grips with matters concerning arbitration. . . . But, I will rest my argument if you will answer me one simple question, namely: Where will I find a comprehensive definition of arbitration?

B... : That's not a fair question, because you know that there is no statutory definition of arbitration. . . . I expect that you are quite aware that one would have to pick around in the court judgments to find bits of a definition to identify arbitration. . . . Which judgments, I accept, are more likely to be
119 defining those procedures which are not arbitration as opposed to those which are. No, I say again, that is not a fair question.

S... : It seems to me to be a very fair question. Perhaps it is the case that what everyone does in the name of arbitration is arbitration; unless it is clearly something else. Perhaps that's a better approach . . . defining what arbitration is not . . . rather than trying to define arbitration itself. . . . I think that **C...** is quite right to say what he did, because it is evident that as soon as one seeks to analyse any aspect of arbitration, there is sufficient confusion about it that it takes massive books to explain it; and yet they only
120 emphasise the confusion.

121 **C...** : Thank you for that support. I shall be a little more outrageous now. . . . Let me put this to you: Is it the case that arbitration was only effective as a procedure for the resolution of disputes all the time that those who used it knew very little about it? . . . Whereas, now that people analyse it in greater and greater depth they simply cause confusion and prevent arbitration being accepted as the obvious procedure. Arbitration could never have had any flexibility at all if people knew precisely, by definition, what it was, could it?

S... : I must agree . . . there can be no flexibility where there is a definitive specification. . . . Unless, of course, the definitive specification merely stated that arbitration is whatever people want it to be. . . . It must be the case that the more definitive the definition of arbitration is, the less flexible
122 it will be. . . . Furthermore, I would say that the more definitive it is, the fewer will be the people who really know the true definition and, thus, only a few people will ever be able to deal with disputes by arbitration; as defined. . . . Perhaps that is why some people are saying that arbitration is falling into decline. . . . By its "analysed definition" it is no longer flexible enough to tackle the disputes that are common everyday occurrences.

A... : Well, that rather deflates all our pragmatic discussions, doesn't it?

S... : Perhaps we do arbitration a disservice by analysing it in the way we do, perhaps we ought to leave it up to the people to do with arbitration as they please . . . to use it in any way they consider appropriate.

123 **B...** : It's odd how the discussion has turned, but the very first Arbitration Act in England concerned voluntary arbitration. . . . It provided the disputants with the opportunity of making their own arbitrations a rule of the court. . . . They had discovered that in situations where the courts had referred cases, initiated in the court, to be dealt with by arbitration, it had contributed much to the ease of the parties. . . . Clearly, there was much voluntary arbitration going on at that time . . . and the degree of flexibility was, no doubt, as wide as the number of people using the procedure. . . . Perhaps it is the case that, since that first Arbitration Act in 1698, the word "flexibility" has always remained the byword of arbitration but . . . the constant process of analysis by the courts and parliament has progressively removed all aspects of flexibility from arbitration; except the expression itself: "flexibility."

C...: I agree . . . .

B...: Moreover, in the process, neither the courts nor parliament have been able to create an arbitration procedure which is clear to all the users. . . . At least, not clear in the way that it must have been clear in the early days of voluntary arbitration . . . which arbitration must have been totally flexible, because it had no definition at all.

S... : Thus, the point made by **C...** is well supported. . . . Now, I must insist that we get back to our main theme and allow **B...** to continue. . . . I am sure we are all satisfied that where both parties know nothing about arbitration, they are not likely to be involved in an arbitration agreement by their own volition, nor are they likely to be concerned about the agreement between the arbitrator and the parties. In any event, if they did, then the chosen arbitrator would have an obvious opportunity to settle his terms of engagement prior to accepting the appointment. . . . And, if the chosen arbitrator did not know about arbitration either . . . well there would be little one could do about it at all. . . . Now, **B...**, can you continue?

B... : Yes. Apart from what I have said about the parties who do not know about arbitration, it is obvious that whenever the parties themselves select an arbitrator, there is an opportunity for the arbitrator and the parties to agree upon the terms of engagement, so with an arbitrator who is aware of the need to include some express terms, there should be no difficulty.

124 **C...** : What about the position where there is to be a tribunal of three, each side choosing one arbitrator and the selected arbitrators agreeing upon a third, how do they sort out the terms of the third arbitrator or, indeed, umpire?

B... : Yes, I was coming to that. There is a further difficulty in so far that each of the parties may reach a separate and totally different agreement about the engagement of each arbitrator. One party may select an arbitrator on terms where liability for negligence is excluded and a fee of £100 per hour is to be paid. The other arbitrator may not trouble about any exclusion agreement and may seek a fee of £200 per hour. Simply put, one may have a tribunal which consists of three people, all with differing terms of engagement. And with each of the terms only being agreed with one side in the case of the arbitrators; and both sides for the umpire. Or there may
125 be a complete mix up where no one has any real understanding at all about the agreement that exists between the tribunal and the parties.

S... : Clearly, that is a most unsatisfactory affair. Please carry on with your next point.

126 **B...** : The next point arises where the arbitrator is appointed by the head person in a professional or trade body. When an arbitrator is appointed, if he accepts the appointment straightaway and proceeds with the arbitration, then . . . there will be no express terms agreed. If, on the other hand, the appointed arbitrator seeks to agree terms and conditions, prior to acceptance, with the parties in dispute, it may be the case that the progress of the arbitration will be frustrated.

S... : Can you relate any more scenarios or is that it?

127 **B...** : It is often the case with arbitrations which are totally administered by

a trade or professional body that all the necessary agreements are in place at the time of the arbitration commencing, so there are no problems there.

S... : Is it your intention to make out a case for all arbitrations to be administered arbitrations, so as to ensure that there will be no problems?

B... : Good Lord, no. Not for one moment. Administered arbitrations serve a purpose, but they could never be flexible enough to handle all the various types of dispute that may arise. It . . . .

C... : Here we have that word again: "flexible."

A... : Many of the administered schemes are really about small consumer
arbitrations. The arrangement is for fixed fees for the arbitrator and simple
128 procedures, mostly based on documents only. It could best be described as
a service because the arbitrator would rarely make very much money out of
it. Nevertheless, some arbitrators achieve a good income by virtually
specialising in small consumer disputes; dealing with many disputes in
sequence. I have heard that some of these arbitrators have done up to ten
or so disputes in a day, and even at modest fees per dispute that can be
quite a good income. However, I understand that some disputes often take
days and the arbitrator earns less in fees than he may normally earn in a
couple of hours.

129 **C...** : Some industries, like shipping and commodities, have the equivalent of administered arbitrations, where all the terms and conditions are set down in advance. The arbitrators are few in number, mostly known to each other, and are usually well aware of the conditions under which they are expected to work. . . . Unlike the construction industry where the whole business of dispute resolution is very much a fragmented situation . . . . I'm sure it's likewise in other industries. It is quite simple to be organised when the centre of the dispute resolution business is based in one central area, like London.

B... : I wish it was as simple as you say, in the circumstances which you describe, but, based on my own experience, there is still much to be desired in the arrangements leading up to the conditions of engagement for arbitrators in all fields of dispute.

P... : Let's stop for lunch at this point, I see that it's ready.

[AFTER LUNCH]

S... : After the general discussion over lunch, it seems to me that there are two courses: (a) That there should be a set of known conditions that will be implied into any arbitration agreement in the absence of express agreement between the parties; and (b) That there should be a set of model conditions available for the parties and the arbitrator to adopt should they have an opportunity of agreeing their own terms prior to the arbitrator's acceptance of the appointment.

A... : And, ideally, both implied and the model should be very much the same.

S... : Of course.

130 **B...** : There are some model conditions in existence at the present time, so there is no point in trying to do that which has already been done.

S... : Can anyone point to a set of model conditions that is completely satisfactory?

131 **B...** : I cannot, but The London Bar Arbitration Scheme's one is comprehensive.

132 **A...** : The Chartered Institute of Arbitrators has got conditions, but they are spread throughout the their various arbitration rules.

C... : I have seen the conditions of several bodies. Generally, they are useful, but often the main points relate to the calculation of cancellation fees; for when an arbitration is concluded prior to an award. . . . But, why don't we set down what we believe should be the implied terms and then they could be specifically adopted with modification where the parties so chose.

A... : I do not believe that you would ever get the backing of statutory force behind any set of implied terms, especially if they were to include an exclusion against claims for negligence. And, if that were the case, it would
133 be dangerous to rely upon implied terms.

B... : That's a good point.

134 **A...** : Of course, the ideal situation would be for everyone who drafts an arbitration agreement, where the arbitrator is to be appointed by the head

person in a professional or trade body, should incorporate, by reference, a set of conditions of engagement for the arbitrator.

B... : That would have to apply to all arbitration agreements, because of the
court's power to appoint an arbitrator. If that were not the case every
135 arbitrator . . . except one appointed by the court . . . would have the benefit
of express conditions of engagement. And that cannot be right.

S... : This is really a complex issue.

C... : It would not be anywhere near so complex if the legislature were to set down a sensible set of parameters for arbitration.

B... : The chances of that are remote, I'm afraid. Arbitration is a private procedure for the resolution of disputes and its salvation is best to be achieved by private means.

S... : So . . . we must find the most suitable means for resolving the issue and hope that all those concerned with the appointment of arbitrators will take heed of the problem and do whatever is necessary in order to bring about the option for there to be agreed terms of engagement for an arbitrator prior to acceptance of the appointment.

136 **A...** : I believe that if those people in positions of authority knew about the problems that existed, they would do something about it.

C... : I wish I had such faith, people are usually in positions of authority because they have become expert at sitting on the fence and not rocking the boat. By the time they are in control, they are so accomplished in the art of not putting a foot wrong, that they avoid all the real issues. On the few occasions when they do something really positive it is usually the wrong thing and they have to do some nifty footwork to retreat.

B... : I wish that I could deny all that you have just said. I would like to, but there is just that element of truth in it that makes what you say plausible.

S... : Let's have more faith and get on with drafting some conditions of engagement and hope that others see the point of including, by reference, something similar into their arbitration agreements.

P... : We've had a good discussion today and have reached a point where it is convenient to close, so let's start afresh tomorrow.

"AGREED"

[10.00 a.m. DAY-5 OF DISCUSSION]

C... : I hope that we can conclude what we are doing today, I have a great deal to attend to when I get back to the office.

S... : I'm sure everyone, bar me, is in the same boat. . . . I suggest that we postpone any discussion on the topic of Third-Parties and Consolidation, even though they concern the parties. We can deal with them on another occasion, such topics are bound to take up some considerable time. . . . The other issues raised are not directly concerned with the relationships between the parties and between the parties and the arbitrator, they are matters of procedure. For example, whether or not the parties have agreed that the procedure shall be inquisitorial or adversarial is irrelevant to the conditions of engagement for the arbitrator. All of these issues we shall leave to a later date. . . . We will attend solely to the conditions of
137 engagement. Let's take each point in turn, consider its purpose, and draft the wording. **B...**, our lawyer, will lead us forward.

138 **B...** : It goes without saying that the agreement must have a heading and I propose the following: TERMS FOR ENGAGEMENT OF THE ARBITRATOR.

A... : I prefer the word "conditions" rather than "terms."

139 **B...** : All stipulations in a contract are "terms." Some of the terms are conditions and some are warranties. So it would be wrong to refer to all the terms as "conditions."

S... : I think that we must be guided by **B...** on these fundamental points. He is the lawyer. I am quite happy for his proposal to go forward.

140 **B...** : Next, we must have the parties identified. I would propose that for clarity and for general use, we have the following: NAME AND ADDRESS OF ARBITRATOR, followed by: NAME AND ADDRESS OF CLAIMANT and likewise: NAME AND ADDRESS OF RESPONDENT. There is no need for witnesses, but some people like to see all documents witnessed, but not I.

C... : Where are the provisions about appointed arbitrators as opposed to one agreed to by the parties; if the terms are to be generally suitable?

B... : If an appointing body adopted the terms as part of the appointing process, then the names of the parties would be entered first and upon appointment the name of the arbitrator would be entered. Any likely

arbitrator who may be appointed would have been required to signal his agreement to the terms prior to an appointment, otherwise he would not be appointed. The parties would know the terms prior to making an application for appointment and the arbitrator would know that, upon his acceptance of the appointment, the terms would be as he had already seen. If the parties sought to deny the terms or impose others, the arbitrator
141 could simply say that he would not be bound by terms other than those known prior to the appointment. . . . The contract between the parties and the arbitrator would be concluded when accepted by the appointed arbitrator. The document signed by the parties would be the offer, and the acceptance by the arbitrator would be absolute and thus a contract concluded.

A... : But . . . what if an appointing body did not adopt the terms as part of the arrangement?

B... : Then, our proposals would be irrelevant. The position would be in the same unsatisfactory situation as at present.

142 **S...** : We have already agreed that we are preparing these terms on the basis of our hope that they will be adopted by appointing bodies or by those who draft arbitration agreements. Our proposed terms may be used also by parties in dispute who select their own arbitrator. . . . Especially once they have been tested in wider debate, which is always an essential part of any such proposal. Please continue.

B... : The next step is to identify the dispute and also the provision giving the power for the matter to be resolved by the particular arbitrator.

A... : Surely, you mean the power to resolve the matter by arbitration and not by the particular arbitrator?

143 **B...** : No. But, I admit I did not express my thoughts very clearly. . . . The parties, by virtue of their having given each other notice to concur in the appointment of an arbitrator, would have commenced the arbitration. Now they need to identify that the arbitrator has been appointed properly.

S... : Quite so, we must be certain that these fine points are taken into account. Please continue.

144 **B...** : The agreement would need only provide a space for these points to be set down. For example: INSERT DETAILS OF THE FOLLOWING: THE SUBJECT OF THE DISPUTE; THE AGREEMENT CONCERNING

THE APPOINTMENT OF THE ARBITRATOR AND HOW THE ARBITRATOR IS TO BE APPOINTED.

C... : If it is just left to the parties, and likely only one party . . . that is, the party who makes the application for the appointment, how will the arbitrator, or anyone else, know that the information has been correctly filled in by the applicant?

S... : That is a very good point, what is the answer to that?

145 **B...** : No problem. One cannot expect the applicant to be an expert, that's true. Neither can one expect that the administration people of the appointing body to be experts, they are basically clerks or administrators. . . . If one believed that the head person in the body, who actually makes the appointment, has the time to really think about such issues, then one is not aware of all the duties that befall such people. So, one must accept that there is a strong likelihood that there may not even be a valid arbitration agreement, let alone that the appointing procedure has been properly followed. . . . So . . . .

C... : It seems that the whole thing is fraught with problems. You started off by saying, "No problem," then you tell us there are so many issues that could arise.

B... : Yes, but, these are all normal issues that have to be faced in dealing with disputes by arbitration. I know that **C...** is simply goading me on this issue, for he knows as well as I do about what the situation is . . . .

S... : Well, my good friend, don't feel goaded, but act as though you were and tell us the position.

146 **B...** : It is the first fundamental step for all arbitrators. They must check the validity of the arbitration clause and also make sure that they have been properly appointed. . . . Part of the business of making sure that a proper appointment has been made is the arbitrator being satisfied that the parties are in dispute.

C...: Then we are back to square-one. We have spoken about the need for an arbitrator to be able to accept the appointment and also to have the conditions . . . sorry . . . terms of engagement already agreed before doing anything and now you tell us that he must check out all sorts of things.

B... : I'm sorry to say that there is so much misunderstanding about these simple preliminary points. . . . I'm appalled by the situation. Let me explain:

If the arbitrator has acceptable terms of engagement in place and has been appointed, once he accepts the appointment he then has all the powers which have been vested in him as arbitrator. Is that agreed?

A... : Yes.

C... : But how will he know what his powers are?

147 **S...** : I don't think we should wander into that quagmire. **B...** has already told us that the total powers of an arbitrator are, in effect, unknown. He has said that the information can only be found by a thorough study of case law, which is always subject to change on a day by day basis. . . . This aspect of arbitration is most unsatisfactory, but there is little we can do about that. However, I believe that **B...** is saying that the powers to do all the things which will arise in his current observations are well settled. Is that correct?

B... : Yes.

148 **C...** : Fine, but this issue of uncertainty in law makes me very angry. Not only is case law subject to change on a day by day basis, but what has already been decided is not totally in accord. It is quite preposterous that ordinary people cannot simply discover these laws which govern their everyday lives. It is simply ludicrous, that trained lawyers are even more confused than ordinary people; because being trained they know even more about the uncertainty of the law. The whole system is the biggest joke of our sophisticated society.

S... : I'm not going to allow anyone to challenge you, this is a very big issue and we must leave if for another time. It is not going to help us resolve the terms of engagement for an arbitration. I must ask you to desist, so that we may make some progress.

B... : I agree, that what **C...** has said is true. He says it more forceably than I would, but it is nevertheless true. The problem is this: Our system may not be perfect, but we had better find something which is infinitely better before we seek to change it.

149 **S...** : Well, that sounds like a good challenge, but a challenge for another day. Now **B...**, will you continue with the points you were making. We are all agreed that, if the arbitrator has acceptable terms of engagement in place and has been appointed, then he has all the powers vested in him, once he accepts the appointment.

150 **B...** : Then by the powers vested in him, his first duty is to satisfy himself about: (a) the validity of the arbitration clause; (b) the validity of his appointment; and (c) that the parties are in dispute. If any doubt exists at all about any of these matters, then the powers which the arbitrator believes that he had would not exist. If the arbitrator discovers that (a) and (b) are in doubt, he may invite both parties to remedy any defect by entering into a new agreement for arbitration and his appointment. But if the parties are not at one on the business of arbitration, then it may be difficult to obtain their agreement. It is often the case that one of the parties, usually the respondent, but not always, will challenge the validity of the arbitration agreement and/or the appointment. If the issues are complex, it may not be possible for the arbitrator to satisfy himself about these issues. He does not
151 have the power to decide the point himself, that is a matter for the court. But, in my opinion, he should always proceed with the arbitration if he is satisfied that these matters are in order. He should leave it up to one of the parties to make an application to the court. . . . He may even adjourn the proceedings pending a decision from the court, but he should never abandon the arbitration unless he is quite satisfied that his appointment is invalid. . . . The important thing is this: That the arbitrator makes it his business to satisfy himself on these points as soon as possible. Sometimes the arbitrator will not be able to tell until after the Points of Claim and the Points of Defence and Counterclaim have been served. Indeed, he may only discover the real situation after the arbitration has progressed a long way. But, the point which I make is this: that he should always be alert to the fact that his appointment may not be valid and he should, immediately after accepting the appointment, take steps to satisfy himself on these points.

S... : And, if the appointment is not valid? . . . What powers did he have in order to commence the proceedings to find out whether or not his appointment is valid?

B... : I believe that the appointed arbitrator, must always be on the alert to find issues that may affect his status. But, as I said: it is correct for him to assume all the powers which he believes he possesses, until such time as he discovers otherwise. The party who sought the invalid appointment may be at risk for costs; if or when the error is discovered. Other parties will have a duty of care to mitigate costs in any event.

152 **A...** : What about an arbitrator who did not, by neglect, discover that his appointment was not valid. Would he have a duty of care to mitigate? Would he be liable for damages?

B... : An interesting point. It touches the very core of the issue of judicial immunity.

153 **S...** : From what you have said, it is much wider than the issue of judicial immunity. If the appointment was valid then judicial immunity would potentially be an issue for an arbitrator. If it was discovered that the appointment was invalid, then the person potentially in the role of an arbitrator would not in fact be an arbitrator at all. Thus, the question of judicial immunity of an arbitrator would not arise. It would in fact be a simple issue of duty of care. So if the person acting as arbitrator did not see that he ought not to be so acting and great costs were incurred as a result, then what would be his liability?

B... : That's a real big issue. I know of no authority on the topic.

S... : It seems that it would be very dangerous for anyone to act as arbitrator unless they had the vision of a god.

B... : We are probably making a mountain out of a molehill.

S... : Even so, I believe that your terms of engagement should cover the point to protect the arbitrator and to warn the parties.

B... : I agree. But before moving on, I would like to deal with the issue (c) about there being an actual dispute. If it turned out that there was no dispute, then as a matter of law, there could be no arbitration. Even if the parties wanted to resolve an issue, they could not make the proceedings an arbitration, simply by calling it arbitration. So it is very important that the
154 arbitrator makes certain that he is dealing with a dispute.

155 **C...** : I hope that you can all see that if the parties do not know much about arbitration and if the arbitrator is equally unaware of things, then what is done in the name of arbitration may not be arbitration. Or alternatively, arbitration is whatever the parties believe it to be and that the more sophisticated one gets in one's study the more arbitration seems to be a nonsense.

S... : I don't think it is wise to get back to that aspect again, we have already covered some of the ground before. I believe the issue is a case of defining what arbitration is; and that has been ruled out of the question. . . . Because we have not been able to produce simple terms which do not need an explanation.

156 **B...** : Quite right. It would never do to explain a term in a contract. It must stand only upon whatever words make up the term. If the explanation is part of the contract, then it becomes part of the terms. If the explanation is outside the terms of the contract, then it has no force.

P... : Thank goodness, it is coffee time. Let's break now.

[POST COFFEE]

S... : It is obvious from what has just been said that when most people speak in precise terms about arbitration, they speak from lack of knowledge. . . . It is quite clear to me that anyone with knowledge of the subject could never speak in a definitive way. . . . So how are we to proceed?

B... : I am certain that it is up to the applicant to answer the questions about the subject of the dispute and the nature of the arbitration agreement. However, I am now convinced that a further term must be included, perhaps in this form: (a) THAT IN ACCEPTING THE APPOINTMENT THE ARBITRATOR RELIES UPON THE APPLICANT'S ASSERTION THAT A GENUINE DISPUTE DOES EXISTS BETWEEN THE PARTIES AND THAT THE DISPUTE IS SUBJECT TO AN ARBITRATION AGREEMENT WHICH PROVIDES FOR AN
157 APPOINTMENT IN THE MANNER SOUGHT; (b) THAT THE APPLICANT SHALL, SO SOON AS IS PRACTICABLE FOLLOWING THE ACCEPTANCE OF THIS APPOINTMENT BY THE ARBITRATOR, SUBMIT PROOF OF THE APPLICANT'S ASSERTIONS; AND (c) THAT THE APPLICANT ACCEPTS FULL RESPONSIBILITY FOR ALL COSTS AND FEES INCURRED BY THE ARBITRATOR AND OF ANY OTHER PARTY ARISING OUT OF ANY ASPECTS SHOULD THERE BE NO SUCH DISPUTE OR NO SUCH ARBITRATION AGREEMENT.

A... : That would deal with the applicant but similar duties should be imposed on the other side.

B... : No. That would not be possible in a contractual sense. If there was a valid arbitration agreement, a valid appointment and a dispute, then the other side would automatically be bound by notice of the arbitration. If these criteria did not exist at all, then the other side would not be bound at all and no obligation could be imposed upon them by a unilateral application. That is why an arbitrator needs to be careful about making certain that the criteria do exist. However, by including the suggested terms, the applicant would be bound to bring forward proof at an early stage and then the arbitrator could make certain that the other party concurred. It there was an objection, then the point could be argued. If there was acceptance, then the arbitrator could make certain that is was recorded that both parties accepted that the criteria was present and thus for practical purposes there would be no problem.

C... : Would it be better for the appointed arbitrator to establish all these things before accepting the appointment?

158 **B...** : Not in my opinion. Because the appointed arbitrator would have no definite powers until he accepted. Nevertheless, if it seems obvious to the potential arbitrator from the details to hand that there may well be some doubt, then enquiries should be made before acceptance. Most of my comments are really related to where the position is not so obvious.

S... : Can you give us an example?

B... : Yes. . . . If the applicant says simply that the respondent owes me £500, then it may well be a simple case of a debt as opposed to a dispute. In which case, the potential arbitrator should enquire about that before acceptance. Whereas, if the applicant says that the respondent owes £500 for delays to the works carried out by the claimant, then on face value there is likely to be a dispute. I am quite satisfied that the terms proposed above will be adequate to put the applicant on his guard.

C... : And, if I may say so, make the potential arbitrator aware of the need to clarify these issues at an early stage.

159 **S...** : Now we must move on. Over coffee, **A...** showed us a set of conditions of engagement which were submitted by a member to the Chartered Institute of Arbitrators some time ago. I believe it may be helpful to set these down and see if we can improve upon them. **A...** says that he has used them himself for many years. Perhaps, if **A...** will read them out, and then **B...** can take up any points for discussion.

B... : I wish we could keep to the expression, Terms of Engagement.

S... : Quite. We shall all refer to your preferred expression.

A... : The terms to which I shall refer are based upon the parties and not the applicant.

B... : That is as it should be. The only aspect of our terms which relate solely to the applicant is about his making a wrongful application because there is no effective arbitration agreement or because there is no dispute. If the terms are to be effective, by allowing the arbitrator to accept the appointment without any more ado, then they must bind all the parties.

S... : Yes, that is the whole point: appointing bodies will only appoint upon certain terms. And, those terms will be incorporated into the arbitration agreement. . . . The parties would be already in agreement that the appointment will be made only on the specified terms. . . . Yes, that is the whole point. Please carry on.

A...: The first part of these terms is about the dispute and the parties and the arbitration agreement. We have already dealt with that part.

B... : Let us call that the premises, now we shall proceed with the terms.

A... : Will the warranty by the applicant be one of the terms?

160 B... : No. That is a warranty which, in effect, is outside the terms which are applicable to both parties and the arbitrator, but it could be also a proviso at the end of the terms.

161 A... : Then I shall use the same numbering and commence with clause 1 which reads: THAT THE PARTIES SHALL BE JOINTLY AND SEVERALLY LIABLE FOR THE FEES AND EXPENSES OF THE ARBITRATOR FROM THE TIME OF THE APPOINTMENT TO THE CONCLUSION OF THE MATTER.

B... : I may seek to suggest alternative wording, but the main thrust is all right. What is next?

162 A... : Clause 2 states: THAT THE PARTIES SHALL BE JOINTLY AND SEVERALLY LIABLE TO TAKE UP THE AWARD OF THE ARBITRATOR BY PAYMENT OF THE ARBITRATOR'S FEES AND EXPENSES WITHIN 14 DAYS OF BEING NOTIFIED OF THE AMOUNT OF SUCH CHARGES AND THAT THE AWARD HAS BEEN PUBLISHED.

163 B... : The Arbitration Act 1950, includes provisions about the payment of the arbitrator's fees under such circumstances and, of course, there is the question that the arbitrator's fees may be taxed by the court.

S... : Is it your position that you believe such a term should not be included?

164 B... : No. I do not see any particular problem with it being included, it is an express term and thus better than an implied term. However, one of the parties may pay the sum demanded into court, instead of paying the arbitrator, and obtain release of the award.

S... : But would you still include that term, or add to it, or delete it?

B... : I would include it.

P... : Then that is a good point to stop for lunch.

[POST LUNCH]

S... : Please continue with the next clause.

165 **A...** : Clause 3 states: THAT IF THE AWARD IS NOT TAKEN UP BY THE PAYMENT OF CHARGES, AS NOTIFIED, THE ARBITRATOR MAY, WITHOUT FURTHER NOTICE, PROCEED AGAINST ANY OR ALL OF THE PARTIES FOR RECOVERY OF COSTS, FEES AND EXPENSES.

B... : Again, it may be useful to include such a term, but it is self-evident that that is the case in any event. I believe that there could be some sharpening up of the wording by using constant expressions. For example, we have "recovery of costs, fees and expenses" here and yet elsewhere we see only "fees and expenses."

A... : Clause 4 states: THAT IF THE AWARD HAS DETERMINED THAT ALL OR ANY PART OF THE COSTS OF THE ARBITRATION SHALL BE PAID BY ANY PARTY OTHER THAN THE PARTY WHICH HAS ALREADY PAID THEM, THAT PARTY SHALL HAVE THE RIGHT TO RECOVER THE APPROPRIATE AMOUNT FROM THAT OTHER PARTY.

166 **B...** : This clause does not relate to the arbitrator and the parties, it's solely about the duty of one party to the other. I do not believe that it should be included within the terms of engagement for the arbitrator.

S... : That must be as you say. There is often a tendency to include many things in contracts which are obvious or which have no bearing upon the parties obligations. I see no reason at all for including the clause.

167 **A...** : Clause 5 states: THAT IF THE PARTIES SHOULD REACH AGREEMENT ON THE MATTERS IN DISPUTE, OR ON TERMINATION OR ABANDONMENT OF THE DISPUTE BEFORE PUBLICATION OF THE AWARD, THEY SHALL EACH BE UNDER AN OBLIGATION TO FORTHWITH NOTIFY THE ARBITRATOR

OF SUCH AGREEMENT, AND SHALL BE JOINTLY AND SEVERALLY LIABLE TO PAY THE PROPER CHARGES OF THE ARBITRATOR AS DUE AT THAT TIME. SUCH CHARGES TO INCLUDE ANY REASONABLE CHARGES IN RESPECT OF THE CANCELLATION OF RESERVED TIME AND COSTS IN RESPECT OF ACCOMMODATION, ETC. WHICH ARE NO LONGER REQUIRED.

168 **B...** : I believe that this clause is essential. But I would wish to see cancellation charges spelt out in detail.

C... : What . . . do you mean rather like liquidated and ascertained damages?

B... : In a way, yes.

C... : I am sorry to say that some arbitrators often seem more interested in cancellation charges than the arbitration itself. I truly believe that some arbitrators wish for the news of cancellation so that they can gain substantial sums of money for doing nothing. They are often able to get on with their normal practice work and make two earnings, one at the expense of the parties in dispute. . . . No, I would rather the arbitrator be limited to claiming only that which is reasonable.

B... : The problem is this: Trying to agree what is reasonable with someone who does not want to pay anything. That situation is fraught with problems of recovery, whereas a simple sum already included within the contract is straightforward.

A... : I have never charged a cancellation fee based upon an agreed schedule. I often wonder about the morals of some the cancellation charges. . . . I've heard about big sums being recovered. I agree with the sentiments expressed by **C...**. The arbitrator is the most joyful of all those involved when hefty cancellation charges have to be paid.

S... : Why can't one have a schedule that sets out a reasonable fee?

B... : The matter is quite simple. If the arbitrator has plenty of other work to do which is not time related, then he may not suffer very much. Whereas, if he relies totally upon previously allocated time for his income, he will totally lose out when time allocated has been cancelled. Most sensibly, the arbitrator should base his losses on the latter. . . . It is better to forewarn
169 the parties about the effect of booking time in advance than shock them at a

later stage when they are trying to reach an agreement only to discover that they owe the arbitrator an unexpectedly high sum.

S... : Clearly there is a problem here. **B...**'s concern is primarily about seeking to recover a reasonable sum as opposed to wanting to be paid a reasonable sum.

C... : **B...**'s concern, like many other people, is about being paid the best sum possible. And, I repeat my concern about the high level of cancellation fees. For evidence, see the way in which cancellations are greeted with such enthusiasm by arbitrators: "I had two arbitrations cancelled last week, so I shall have a paid holiday." is typical of the comments I've heard.

B... : I'm not going to rise to the bait.

C... : Commercial arbitrators have learnt the skills of barristers and learnt about their Brief fees. . . . I've yet to find a case settled prior to the barristers being paid the Brief fees. Often the cases have settled very soon after, which means that the Brief fee is secured and very little is done.

B... : That's absolute rubbish.

S... : As I said, there is clearly a problem here. It cannot be wrong to seek to recover a reasonable sum, so let's leave the clause much as it stands. In any event, if the terms of engagement are going to be accepted generally, then it would not be easy to set down a schedule of damages for cancellat-
170 ion of the arbitration.

A... : If arbitrators continually advised the parties about the fees being incurred and about what the reasonable sum was likely to be in the event of a cancelled hearing, there should be little difficulty. I believe it is quite wrong for the parties to be unaware about costs until a total sum is known at the end. . . . I always keep the parties briefed on my progressive costs. But I find it difficult to get the parties to do the same, they seem most reluctant to provide details about the progressive amount of costs being incurred. I'm sure it would be beneficial for the costs to be disclosed and
171 monitored throughout the entire arbitration. I'm sure that it would benefit the procedure generally and, moreover, specifically help the parties to realise the need to proceed in the most effective manner. I wish that I had the power to make orders for the parties to disclose their progressive costs to each other and to the arbitrator.

B... : That would never do. . . . Such an order would force the parties to disclose their strategy for proceeding with the dispute. It may well limit the power of a skilled lawyer to extract the best terms when negotiating a settlement or, for example, when making a sealed offer. It is essential that the opposing party is kept guessing about expected liability, including costs, otherwise where would be the power in the sealed offer?

C... : A very good question. . . . And, if I may say so, an honest disclosure which identifies much about what is wrong with arbitration.

B... : In what way?

C... : First, there should be no question of strategy. The parties should come before the commercial arbitrator with a willing desire to settle a dispute in private because they are desirous of avoiding the cut and thrust of litigation
172 in the public arena.

B... : You seek utopian concepts for arbitration. It would never be the case between conflicting parties.

173 **C...** : I'm quite sure that one of the major problems with arbitration is this: That the experts, the lawyers and the arbitrators all assume that the parties are seeking more than a simple resolution of a conflict. Often, in my own personal experience, all that the parties wanted was a resolution of a conflict in the most effective way. . . . What they got was simply the creation of a game of strategy and conflict about procedural rules brought about by the desires and interests of their advisers. In arbitration, the only conflict should be the dispute and nothing else.

174 **B...** : Your desires are created by thoughts derived out of fantasy. Disputes are disputes. And every angle of fighting the battle must be explored in the interests of one's client. There is no other way.

C... : That is the way of litigation. That's why people turned to arbitration. Now, it seems, it is becoming the way of arbitration. That's why people seek
175 some other alternative, like ADR. . . . When ADR becomes the next procedure to suffer from the experts on strategy, and from all those who seek to take advantage of the disadvantaged, again, the people in dispute will look elsewhere. And, do you know where they will look?

B... : No. Where?

176 **C...** : Simple. They will look towards litigation, because in the end, the only tribunal which will have the power to root out strategy, will be the judge in litigation. Mark my words, they are doing it already, that is why many

people are turning back to litigation. The whole thing is turning the full circle.

177 **A...** : The Official Referee's court is a good example of that, the judges there get most impatient with any form of strategy. I've got a feeling the we have only just seen the beginning of that court reaching its full potential.

S... : Well . . . this is all most interesting and will surely provide us with much to talk about in the future, but we must keep to the task in hand. Let's move on to the next clause.

C... : I think we should return to that aspect soon, I wish one could make such a philosophy part of the terms . . . do you agree?

B...: No, is my simple response.

S...: Let's move on.

178 **A...** : Clause 6 states: THAT THE ARBITRATOR REQUIRES SECURITY IN THE SUM OF £__________ BEFORE PROCEEDING WITH THE REFERENCE, AND THAT SUCH SECURITY SHALL, AT THE DETERMINATION OF THE ARBITRATOR, BE INCREASED FROM TIME TO TIME AS THE ARBITRATION PROCEEDS. SUCH SECURITY TO BE PLACED IN THE HANDS OF THE CHARTERED INSTITUTE OF ARBITRATORS TO HOLD AS STAKE HOLDER PENDING SUBMISSION OF INTERIM AND FINAL ACCOUNTS FOR FEES AND EXPENSES AT ANY REASONABLE TIME WITHIN THE SOLE DISCRETION OF THE ARBITRATOR. THE ARBITRATOR SHALL NOTIFY ALL PARTIES, BY COPY INVOICE, OF ANY CHARGES SENT TO THE STAKE HOLDER.

B... : Because of our view about the arbitrator being in the position to accept an appointment without having to negotiate with the parties first, then the wording needs changing. But in general the clause is essential. Three other points: (a) the Chartered Institute does not have hands; (b) the party who provided the security should have the original invoice; and (c) it is not possible to have "any reasonable time within the sole discretion of the arbitrator." It is either at the discretion of the arbitrator or it's "any reasonable time."

S... : It could be both as a matter of fact.

B... : Yes, but not as a matter of requirement.

S... : Could the arbitrator exercise his discretion in an unreasonable way?

B... : No. No. I don't mean it like that. I'm referring to the drafting only. If the action is to be at the discretion of the arbitrator, then it is implied that his discretion will be exercised reasonably.

A... : "Should be"?

B... : No. "Will be" exercised.

S... : Do you wish to redraft the clause now?

179 **B... :** It's an important clause, so I will let you have a draft. We must make it clear that if the applicant does not put up security, then the arbitrator will not be bound by his acceptance of the appointment. If all parties share the security that would be up to them. But, the applicant must understand that he may be called upon to provide security for all the arbitrator's fees and costs right up to the conclusion of the arbitration. And, in the event of failure, the arbitrator will not be bound to proceed.

A... : So you are saying that if the applicant runs out of money at the end of the hearing and cannot afford to put up enough security to cover the preparation of the award, then the arbitrator can just stop work on the case?

B... : Precisely, and that's how it should be. Why should the arbitrator stand at risk?

180 **C... :** I believe that is fair. It would always be up to the respondent to volunteer to put up security, but the applicant should always be prepared to fund the arbitrator. I agree that the arbitrator should not be put to work without knowing that his fees and costs are secure.

A... : I usually seek both parties to pay up in equal shares. I think that's fair and there is no sense of bias.

B... : If you are implying that an arbitrator would be biased in his orders and his award simply because only the applicant put up security, then that would be a very sorry state of affairs.

A... : No. An arbitrator should not be biased. . . . He . . . .

S... : You do not seem to be certain on the point. Perhaps you think that some may be biased if only the applicant put up security.

181 **C...** : Let's save **A...** from having to speculate on that point. If the respondent believed that an arbitrator was biased, for any reason, then he could apply to the court to have him removed, but the respondent had better have a better case than simply showing that the claimant had to put up all the security in order to get the arbitrator to proceed.

B... : That must be so.

P... : Then let us pause for a break.

[POST BREAK]

S... : I did not think that a break for refreshment would end discussion on that last topic, but we must now press on.

182 **A...** : Clause 7 states: THAT THE ARBITRATOR'S FEES WILL BE CHARGED AT £_________ PER HOUR/DAY IN RESPECT OF ALL TIME SPENT UPON THE ARBITRATION AND ALSO ANY TRAVELLING TIME; TOGETHER WITH ALL EXPENSES FOR TRAVEL, SUBSISTENCE, HIRE OF ARBITRATION ROOMS, POSTAGE, TELEX, CABLE, TELEPHONE, COPYING, RECORDING, TYPING, TRANSCRIBING, REPORTS OF EXPERTS AND ADVISORS, AND ANY OTHER LIKE ITEMS ALL CHARGEABLE AT COST. IN ADDITION, VAT WILL BE ADDED AT THE APPROPRIATE RATE.

C... : These terms must be out of date, because there is no mention of FAX.

A... : The principles are the same and require no amendment as a result of time alone.

S... : I agree, there is always a tendency to keep starting from scratch every time. We must be sure to build upon that which we have already. But, of course, we must be prepared to demolish completely that which is no longer needed.

B... : This clause would not fit in with the idea of the arbitrator accepting the appointment prior to recourse to the parties. The arbitrator would not have a unilateral power to impose a specific fee rate upon the parties.

A... : That may create a problem as many arbitrators would not wish to start an arbitration without something agreed. I've always found parties ready to agree to my fees.

C... : Perhaps that's because your fees are modest.

A... : Perhaps, but that fact alone must be of some importance.

183 **B...** : It all comes down to this: If the arbitrator will not accept the appointment until his fees are agreed and if the parties do not jointly accept the fees, then the arbitration is frustrated.

S... : Then how can we overcome that problem.

B... : You can't.

S... : Then all our work is wasted. Perhaps we should have started with fees first. We would have saved much time.

C... : This dilemma is present in all aspects of disputes. It high-lights the need for parties to be in accord in dealing with their disputes by arbitration. However, on the assumption that we are not going to throw overboard the procedure of arbitrators being appointed by an independent person, we must find a way of resolving this big issue. It is quite wrong that one party is able to frustrate the procedure by adopting a strategy of not agreeing to the arbitrator's fees. . . . But, I have greater faith in the system, and I believe that most parties would be happy to agree fees. . . . The issue is whether the arbitrator is in control before fees are agreed or whether he will take no action until his fees are agreed. Providing the arbitrator is secured for reasonable fees, I believe that the arbitrator should go ahead and be
184 content with reasonable fees, which can be taxed by the court.

S... : Then how do you overcome the problem of drafting the clause?

C... : **B...** would obviously be better at drafting, but I would suggest that the arbitrator makes a statement about his fees. For example, the terms could be in this form: That the fees of the arbitrator shall be a reasonable fee based upon the complexity of the dispute, the time taken, the skill required, etcetera, together with all disbursements, much the same as the clause quoted by **A...** a few moments ago. . . . Then, there could be a statement like
185 this: That the arbitrator normally charges a fee of £____________ per hour/day and the parties are invited to accept that fee.

S... : Can you do something on those lines, **B...**?

B... : Yes. I would turn it about. I would start with the invitation and then state that if the fee was not agreed by both parties, then the basis of charge will be . . . a reasonable fee, etcetera.

S... : Please draft something for consideration.

186 **A...** : In fact, although many arbitrators say that they seek agreement before they start, it's my belief that many of them start before such agreement and, indeed, they are improperly giving orders and setting up meetings without the authority of an arbitrator. The proposals by **C...** will help to go a long way towards resolving this issue and any arbitrator who does not like the idea should not offer to accept appointments from appointing bodies.

S... : What is the next clause?

187 **A...** : Clause 8 states: THAT THE ARBITRATOR'S FEES WILL BE SUBJECT TO REVIEW AT SIX MONTHLY INTERVALS FROM THE DATE OF THE THIS AGREEMENT.

B... : This term should be incorporated within the previous one. Here again, there is no way that the arbitrator could impose the amount of any increase at the end of six months. He would have a right to review, but the amount could not be imposed unilaterally.

S... : We will leave it to you to merge the two clauses. What is next?

188 **A...** : Clause 9 states : [EXCLUSION OF LIABILITY] THAT THE ARBITRATOR DECLINES ABSOLUTELY TO ACCEPT THE RISKS OF HAVING TO DEFEND A NEGLIGENCE CLAIM AND HE SHALL NOT BE LIABLE FOR ANY ACT OR OMISSION IN, OR IN CONNECTION WITH, THIS ARBITRATION. THIS ABSOLUTE EXCLUSION OF LIABILITY EXTENDS TO ALL MATTERS EXCEPT ANY CONSCIOUS AND DELIBERATE WRONGDOING ON THE PART OF THE ARBITRATOR.

S... : This seems like a big issue.

A... : It is.

B... : It is just a matter of policy, either the arbitrator has judicial immunity or he doesn't. There is nothing in the statutes about the issue and the judgments of the courts have always fostered the idea that an arbitrator may not have the immunity, but they have always tipped the scales slightly in favour of immunity.

S... : That seems to be most unsatisfactory.

B... : It is, but lawyers, and especially judges have the same problem as the rat catcher; who always manages to miss the pregnant rat, thus ensuring a continuing flow of work for the future.

C... : Did I hear you correctly? Did you really say that, or was I simply have one of my usual daydreams.

B... : I was only having a little joke at the expense of lawyers.

C... : I expect that **B...** had an unguarded moment, whilst in the company of friends, and a little bit of his subliminal thinking escaped to the surface. All that he said, I believe to be true.

189 **S...** : The example given was simply one of human nature. There is a great reluctance on the part of anyone to close all the issues finally, because they may need an escape route themselves. It seems that there is some merit in always keeping a foot in the door, whatever one's job. However, there are fortunately some of us who are anxious to see unnecessary obscurities removed from the procedure. So, let us have some comments on the term.

B... : I would certainly delete the last sentence from the clause, because it is obvious that it must be the case. If it were left in, any lawyer could use it as a springboard for an action.

C... : Leaving it in may give the parties some comfort in knowing that the arbitrator recognises that he would not be immune from proceedings in respect of conscious and deliberate wrongdoing.

B... : My advice would be to leave it out.

S... : But are we all agreed that the main point of the exclusion should remain in?

190 **B...** : Until such time that the courts, or the legislature, sort themselves out on the matter, it will provide some protection by an express term.

S... : I must say that I expected some considerable debate on this point.

A... : I believe that most of us are in agreement that the arbitrator should have judicial immunity. A survey of the members of the Chartered Institute of Arbitrators indicated that seventy per cent of those responding consid-
191 ered that arbitrators should have the same judicial immunity as a judge.

C... : I would go further. . . . In considering the position of the arbitrator and his need to be unbiased, he ought to have absolute immunity. A judge is employed by the state and has the entire backing of the establishment behind him, whereas an arbitrator is alone and isolated, just an individual. I would not wish to see him worried about such things when dealing with one of my disputes. It is not in anyone's interest, to make the arbitrator insecure and afraid of his position on the question of claims for negligence. The judiciary and the government are foolish to play around with the issue.

192 A... : There are some people who believe that an arbitrator will attend more properly to matters and make certain that he is the right man for the job, if he knows that he will be liable for negligence.

C... : If that were the case, then in other professions we would find that there would be no claims for negligence, because they do not have immunity. Such arguments are irrelevant to the situation. Are we to have parties suing an arbitrator after an award, or even during a hearing, on their own unilateral motion, just as it takes their fancy?

193 B... : The courts have extensive powers to remove arbitrators and to correct awards, so there is no need to rely upon negligence claims, except, of course, for damages. That's the nub of the problem, the parties may have expended large sums and then discover that they have a bum arbitrator. However, I believe that the parties must satisfy themselves about the arbitrator. That is another good reason for a mutual desire of the parties to go to arbitration; which would allow the parties to choose the right arbitrator and settle all the terms. And, of course, our idea of "a pause" after the appointment would be invaluable in this respect.

S... : So about the term?

B... : If arbitrators have immunity then we don't need the term. If they do not, then we do need the term and, perhaps, professional indemnity cover as well. . . . I don't know what a judge is likely to do if the matter comes before the court. . . .Although, I personally believe the judicial immunity exits, I would still keep the clause in. . . . Whether I would advise on professional indemnity cover, I cannot tell. If, however, I was giving advice to a client, I would be bound to protect my own interest first and say that it would be wise to have professional indemnity cover, just in case. Otherwise, I may be sued for giving bad advice and my own P.I. premium may go up as
194 a result.

C... : That is just about the measure of the whole matter, isn't it?

195 **S...** : I'm afraid so. An arbitrator who looks after his own interest for fear of action being taken against him, is no use to anyone. We all know about professional men who, in the back of their mind, always have their own interest first when taking any action. An arbitrator faced with such fears would develop a natural cunning in protecting himself. It would probably manifest itself in the arbitrator allowing the parties to make all the running and being himself careful not to put a foot wrong.

C... : That's the growing problem with arbitration. An arbitrator must be allowed to act impartially, not just between the parties to the dispute, but also between himself and the parties. The latter being the most important; because if he takes himself into account he does so in total secrecy, no one but himself knowing. Whereas, if he is biased as between the parties, he must show his hand, even if the hand is shown only by an award which one party believes is biased. The award is published to both parties and can be challenged in the courts, as indeed, can all aspects of procedure. . . . But,
196 we can never challenge the secret thoughts of an arbitrator, never. We will create a very unsatisfactory situation if ever arbitrators can be sued in negligence. Their first duty will be to themselves and their insurance companies; a situation which is totally alien to the concept of arbitration.

S... : I agree. . . . What other clauses do we have?

A... : Clause 10 is about the rules to be adopted for the arbitration procedure.

B... : That is a matter for the parties to agree and not the arbitrator. I do not think it should be one of the terms.

197 **S...** : This whole document can be attached to the back of our notes, for reference purposes. . . . Is that the end?

A... : The last item is the space for each of the parties to sign the agreement, together with provision for the signatures of witnesses.

B... : Space for signing is, of course, essential. I have already said that I do not think that witnesses are necessary.

S... : Is that the last point then?

A... : There are some points about the right of an arbitrator to retire from a reference owing to delay.

198 **B...** : That has been dealt with in the Courts and Legal Services Act 1990.

199 **A...** : I, for one, am not very satisfied with that provision. I would like an express provision on the lines of the Miller proposal which would allow the arbitrator to retire from a reference where the parties cause or allow excessive delays beyond anticipated dates. An anticipated date could be included, by the applicant, in the agreement.

B... : But, what if the applicant misjudged the situation, or if the respondent disagreed?

A... : That is a good point, but somehow I believe we must find a way of dealing with the issue. It would not be the intention that the parties to the dispute lost their rights to settle their dispute. But, I do believe that when it is anticipated that an arbitration will take six months, or twelve, that the arbitrator should be able to say that this arbitration is just dragging on and I intend to resign and leave you to proceed either in litigation or in another arbitration. It is just not good enough to bind an arbitrator to a dispute for an indefinite time. He is an individual and it is quite unreasonable to expect such commitment on the instigation of the parties alone. I'm not suggesting that every arbitrator would wish to resign, but where there is genuine cause for resignation owing to the intransigence of the parties and the inability of the arbitrator to continue with the matter, then something should be done.

B... : That's a very big issue. What about fees and costs already incurred?

A... : I'm not anxious to minimise the problems and I cannot give an answer on the question of fees. But, if a judge in the court cannot carry on then another will be found. And if the case drags on, the judge does not have to keep looking at the file on the shelf. When the matter arises, say one party seeks to have the matter terminated for delay, whatever judge is available will attend to the matter. But with arbitration this is not the case.

200 **S...** : **A...** does have a point. Perhaps **B...** will draft something for consideration. We must all remember that the product of our five days of discussion will be simply a draft, which will be made available for wider discussion. It is not our intention to produce the definitive words upon the relationship between the parties and between the arbitrator and the parties. We have done what we intended. We have identified some of the problems, we have proposed some solutions. Hopefully the issue will get the wider debate that it deserves. We must now leave that for others.

C... : I know that I speak for all present when I say that much has been learnt by us all over these five days. We have not become more certain about things. Indeed, we have become more aware that any concepts held about certainties in arbitration are totally misplaced. I shall look forward to hearing about the date of our next discussion when we can gather together again, in friendship, and discuss some of the issues left over from the instant discussion and also cover some fresh topics.

A... : Here, here!

B... : I will pass my notes and suggestions over to our good friend **P...** who has set patiently making notes. However, I wish - like arbitration - that these discussions were private. I fear we may all suffer some degree of ridicule from our colleagues when they see **P...**'s notes. But, we knew the rules when we started and I accept that our very words will be reproduced; good or bad: the product of wisdom or the exposure of incompetence.

P... : Who will be so harsh as to criticise you, you who have expressed your concerns and offered your thoughts on these topics? Nevertheless, I'm pleased to have been the note-taker only.

THE NOTES

1. There is no intention to infer that the speaker came up from Hades!

2(a). As far as I can determine, there has been very little parliamentary debate in the House of Commons at any time during the twentieth century on issues concerning arbitration. For example, the Arbitration Act 1979 was introduced as a Bill in the House of Lords on the 12th December 1978. This Bill followed on from The Commercial Court Committee's *Report on Arbitration*, of July 1978, Cmnd. 7284; a fairly brief document with very few references or background papers. It is well known that the Bill was squeezed in during the last days of the presiding government. During the few hours of the Bill being considered in Committee, on the 2nd April 1979, concern was expressed at the lack of time. Mr. Michael Neubert, MP for Romford stated, "I should put it on record that the Bill, in the circumstances of the Government's defeat last Wednesday, comes before us unexpectedly soon and comes before a Committee of the whole House rather than the more intimate and leisurely proceedings of a Standing Committee. For this reason, it has taken by surprise many of those most closely interested in its provisions. Only this morning, I received three letters of substance on the Bill all dated last Friday and all expressing concern that the Bill should not be rushed through while it remained unamended in several important respects." It is pertinent to note that some twelve years after these brief debates, Lord Justice Steyn, Chairman of the Department of Trade and Industry's Departmental Advisory Committee on Arbitration, said this about the Arbitration Act 1979: "It was hastily enacted legislation. In their spare time some of their Lordships [Law Lords] were apparently involved in the drafting of that statute. It is, however, not a conspicuously well drafted statute. Fortunately, when their Lordships returned to their constitutional role of deciding concrete cases, they succeeded by and large in making the 1979 Act work satisfactorily . . ." [*(1992) 58, JCIArb 2*, p. 84.]

2(b). The Arbitration Act 1950 was an Act to Consolidate the Arbitration Acts, 1889 to 1934 and, so, there was very little debate necessary for that Act to be passed. The Consolidation Bill was introduced in the Lords and considered in Committee by the Commons. On the 28th July 1950, it was noted that the Committee had reported on the Bill without amendment and it was read a Third time. Mr. Scholefield Allen, MP for Crewe, stated: "As a lawyer, I should like to welcome these consolidation Measures. I think a very good job has been done. It was a job which required doing. It will be of great help to the legal profession and will give help to the public." The Bill was accordingly read a Third time and passed without amendment.

2(c). In 1936, the Lords introduced a short Arbitration Bill, Which Lord Asquith said, "[was a Bill] to prevent parties to contracts from acting as umpires or arbitrators; in fact, to prevent a person being an arbitrator in his own cause." [Hansard, 9th December 1936, col 709.] The Secretary of State for Air, Viscount Swinton, advised the Lords that he could not give any guarantee that the Bill would get through another place. He stated, "Your Lordships know what a very heavy programme the Government have put before Parliament and I could not possibly give a guarantee of that kind." [Ibid, col. 720.]

2(d). So it would seem that even if MPs' desired to take a real interest in arbitration statutes, they are mostly deprived of the opportunity. Perhaps that is what needs to be addressed.

3. Plato, in book XII, 938, of *The Laws* considered "Unscrupulous Advocacy," and stated: "Take justice . . . which has civilised so much of our behaviour: how could it fail to be a blessing to human society? And, granted justice is a blessing, can advocacy fail to be a blessing too? But valuable though they are, both these institutions have a bad name. There is a certain kind of immoral practice, grandly masquerading as a 'skill,' which proceeds on the assumption that a technique exists - itself, in fact - of conducting one's own suits and pleading those of others, which can win the day regardless of the right and wrongs of the individual case; and that this skill itself and the speeches composed with its help are available free - free, that is, to anyone offering a consideration in return." [Trevor J. Saunders' translation, Penguin Classics.]

4. The first Edition of *Russell on Arbitration* was published in 1849, the twentieth edition is current at the present time. Until the publication of *Commercial Arbitration*, by Mustill & Boyd, "Russell" was considered the standard work. Now most people seem to refer first to Mustill & Boyd's' book, which is currently in its second edition. That is not intended to imply that "Russell" has lost its value, only that the "in" book is *Commercial Arbitration*, by Mustill & Boyd.

5(a). There is a substantial body of opinion that supports the concept that arbitrators should be able to decide matters on the basis of what is just and fair. [See the author's booklet, *Arbitration - Recommendations & Survey*, (Herne Bay: Ruthtrek, 1988), ISBN 0 9514295 0 7, question 1.01, p. 37, where two-thirds of responders supported the concept.]. However, anyone who holds the belief that an arbitrator should have the power to make an award on this basis regardless of the parties wishes would have completely misunderstood the whole basis of arbitration; which is fulfilling the arbitration agreement made between the parties. The real problem facing the parties who seek an award based on "*ex aequo et bono*," is that such an award will not be enforceable under the Arbitration Acts. Stewart Boyd, QC., in his paper "'Arbitrator not to be bound by the Law' Clauses," presented at *The Ronald Bernstein Lectures 1989*, stated: ". . . from the beginning of the nineteenth century, the courts consistently followed a course of holding the arbitrator to a rigid application of the law in making his award. . . ." The purpose of his paper was, of course, to promote the case for arbitrator's awards based on equity clauses to be enforceable through the courts. See also 108.

5(b). The recommendation made in, *Arbitration - Recommendations & Survey*, P. 5, was this: "That there should be a statutory provision to allow the parties to expressly agree, in writing after the dispute has arisen, that it is their intention that the arbitrator shall make an award on whatever basis seems fair to the arbitrator and such agreement shall have the same effect as the parties entering into an exclusion agreement under s. 3 of the Arbitration Act 1979."

6. See 49.

7. As at 1992/93 there were 14 lawyers per 10,000 of the population in England and Wales, see the *Law Society's Annual Statistical Report.* In the USA the proportion is higher. Perhaps some reader will know the proportion of lawyers in some of the grief-stricken areas of the world: I merely speculate that it will be low compared to the figure quote above.

8. See 9, below, and 34.

9. Section 32 of the Arbitration Act 1950 makes it clear that an arbitration agreement must be in writing in order to come within the scope of the arbitration statutes. Any arbitration which does not come within the scope of the arbitration statutes, e.g., an arbitration based on an oral agreement, is likely to be a common law arbitration; see Halsbury's Laws, para. 608: "An oral agreement is valid only if it relates to an existing dispute and incomplete until the appointment of the arbitrator, and the arbitrator's authority to conduct the arbitration can be revoked at any time before the publication of the award."

10. Documentary evidence about the lack of knowledge held by the parties is limited because arbitration is a private procedure. But there is so much oral anecdotal evidence passed around by arbitrators - and others in the business of dispute resolution - about the lack of knowledge possessed by parties involved in the process, that I do not expect anyone will challenge the point made. I believe that if someone wishes to argue the alternative, they would need to argue against the face of human nature in the aspect of learning and acquiring knowledge. Experience is, of course, by definition, knowledge gained during the event and assessed post the event. Other forms of learning are based primarily on a "need to know." And very few people other than arbitrators, lawyers, expert witnesses, etc. perceive a "need to know" about arbitration prior to a dispute arising. Further, if anyone should doubt the ignorance of the parties, they would certainly challenge the observations about solicitors as expressed by Clifford Evans. Evans is a well known arbitrator and a member of the Council of the Chartered Institute of Arbitrators. He expressed in writing that which many others have said privately: "The majority of disputes are taken to court by solicitors who have very little knowledge or experience of arbitration. . . . I know many solicitors who know little about arbitration and therefore do not recommend it to their clients as a method of settling disputes." [*ARBITRATION*, Journal of the Chartered Institute of Arbitrators, May 1987, p. 140.] Evans urged that solicitors be formally educated in the business of arbitration. His desires are being fulfilled and the Chartered Institute of Arbitrators' ranks have swollen with the increasing numbers of solicitors, and barristers, who seek to know more about arbitration. But the point I make is this: If Evans is right about solicitors, then surely I am right about the lack of knowledge held by the parties.

11. Robert Coulson, sometime President of the American Arbitration Association ("AAA"), in his book, *Business Arbitration - What you need to know*, (New York, AAA, Third Edition, 1987, at page 43) wrote: "The mini-trial is a structured dispute resolution method in which senior executives of the parties involved in legal disputes meet in the presence of a neutral advisor and, after hearing presentations of the merits of each side of the dispute, attempt to formulate a voluntary settlement." The USA is the birth-place of the mini-trial. Coulson's

book sets out the process as developed by the AAA and also provides a useful bibliography of other pertinent written material on the topic.

12(a). ADR - Alternative Dispute Resolution - is a generic term for all forms of dispute resolution other than litigation. For example, mini-trials are part of the ADR repertoire. The ADR term was developed is the USA, but the repertoire is really all those tried and trusted procedures for dispute resolution that have existed for many years, but which have in recent times required rejuvenation. This rejuvenation process has gathered apace with the promotion of the concepts under the title of ADR. The various procedures have been identified and the formulations set down as guidelines. In the USA all procedures which are not litigation are termed ADR including arbitration. For example *The Alternative Newsletter*, edited by Professor James B. Boskey for the The Association of American Law Schools, includes arbitration as part of ADR [Newsletter available from its editor at Seton Hall Law School, 1 Newark Place, Newark, NJ 07102.]. Whereas CEDR, the Centre for Dispute Resolution, in the United Kingdom, regard ADR as being alternative to litigation and arbitration. No doubt because of the view expressed by some that arbitration has become simply a mirror image of litigation. Details of the work of CEDR are obtainable from 3/5 Norwich Street, London, EC4A 1EJ.

12(b). Any advancement of the public's awareness of all the forms of dispute resolution procedure is invaluable. This is especially so in the case of all procedures which are alternative to litigation. Before a dispute is allowed to turn the parties into unrelenting - and often bitter - adversaries, it is wise to explore the procedures of conciliation, mediation, mini-trial or, indeed, any other process that may lead to a satisfactory settlement. For there are so many facets in the whole business of human tolerance in the face of differences that may exist between people and each facet should be explored. The facets of the crystal are worth turning around often to see whether they catch the rays of light in a way more pleasing to those who look upon it. But as with a crystal, no matter how it be turned, it will never give off the same reflection to separate pairs of eyes; be the crystal held by one or many hands. Thus, with dispute resolution: the whole problem of any procedure which does not rely upon enforcement, is that it has to rely upon each party seeing a reflection from the facet which is the most pleasing [or least upsetting] for there to be a resolution; it is unlikely that the potential settlement will, in fact, be the same to all parties; but it is enough that they each believe it to be so [Subject, of course, to the "belief" not being the product of deception by one party or total ignorance on the part of the other; that outcome would be the product of immorality or perhaps even fraud.]. The parties have to be brought towards a settlement which can for them be seen as common ground; or at the very least a settlement which both parties can accommodate without further desire to seek retribution.

13. The statement in the text seems to state the obvious [see 10. supra.], but the obvious is so often forgotten by those who draft arbitration bills and the rules for procedure. It is also a neglected factor that many arbitrators have no specific training. And, it is no particular answer to counter that observation with the remark that only competent arbitrators ought to be

arbitrators; unless, of course, the counter is coupled with the notion that only suitably qualified people ought to be arbitrators. If the latter were to be the case, then the job of arbitrator would need to be a registered profession; and that would certainly change the entire face of arbitration from what it has been known since records exist. Mustill & Boyd make the point extremely well in their book, *The Law and Practice of Commercial Arbitration in England*, where they state: "If the parties choose to have their disputes resolved by a person who is not equal to the task, they must abide by their choice. Extreme youth or age, mental or physical infirmity, do not deprive an arbitrator of the power to act, or render his award a nullity." (Second Edition, p. 247.)

14. It seems to be a simple fact of life that most people do not study the contracts before signing them. *The Times*, 12th December 1990, referred to a most apposite statement: "Words of wisdom from, of all places, a Florida newspaper: *The difference between education and experience is really quite simple. Education is what you get from reading the fine print. Experience is what you get from not reading it.*" Even the most experienced commercial people do not seem to study the small print. Sometimes it is studied carefully in respect of the actual undertakings of the parties, but even where an arbitration agreement is known about, to become an expert on dispute resolution - litigation or arbitration - as well as being a commercial man, is simply to expect too much. See also 41.

15. It is quite possible for there to be people who volunteer to provide a service free of charge, but generally it is right to assume that any service provided to assist with dispute resolution is done at the expense of the parties, of some trade body, of some charity, or funded by the government. Some one somewhere has to pay. However, it may not be quite true to say that, "no form of dispute resolution will ever be economical for the people in dispute."

16. There is often a tendency to allow oneself the luxury of believing that people generally know about something when in fact the opposite is true. It is only when a law is in accord with the general nature of peoples' thinking that there is any likelihood of general knowledge and the law being compatible; and that's not likely to be very often in procedural issues of dispute resolution; which procedure is likely to be quite alien to people generally; that is, until the logic is explained in some detail; even then, with knowledge of the reasons for the procedure, all that is likely is that people will fall into different classes: namely, those who favour an inquisitorial procedure or adversarial; those who favour discovery, those who don't; etcetera.

17. See article, F.E.Miller, "Redefining terms of arbitration," *New Law Journal*, June 8, 1990. Where it is argued that arbitration must be either defined or, alternatively, treated as a "word of art."

18. See 10.

19. This is a remark which I have often heard. There is a tendency for some to believe that if the parties are not locked into arbitration they will try and avoid the procedure. The belief, I am sure, is a fallacy. But, if the view were not held generally, then why should there such a desire

to tie people to arbitration long before they are likely to be in dispute? There is not likely to be much in the way of written evidence to support such a statement. See 46. for potential losers.

20. See 12.

21. Dr. John Phillips in his book, *Arbitration Law and Practice*, refers to arbitration from early Egyptian times and points to specific records still in existence from the Pie Powder Courts of the thirteenth century. So there is every reason to believe that the concept will survive.

22. Even the courts were the centre of activity as can be seen from Plato's Apology 26E, where he describes the court at the trial of Socrates as having a tribunal of 501 people.

23. The state courts are the only effective default procedure because they have the power to enforce the decision of their judges. No other procedure can claim to have such a legitimate power.

24. Every arbitration agreement which is included in a standard form of contract is, in part, an attempt to make arbitration the default procedure. Every attempt to limit the courts' supervision of arbitration is an attempt to make arbitration the default procedure. Such attempts to make arbitration free-standing are commonplace.

25. In *Bremer Vulcan v. South India Shipping*, [1981] 1 All ER 289, Lord Diplock was concerned with a case about delay in an arbitration, which delay the High Court and the Court of Appeal had decided as a matter of fact was inordinate: Lord Fraser of Tullybelton stated: "We must, I think, accept the concurring findings of the Commercial Court [Donaldson J.] and the Court of Appeal [Lord Denning MR, Roskill and Cumming-Bruce LJJ] that the delay was such as to prevent a fair hearing, and that if the claim had been made in an action it would have been dismissed for want of prosecution," [1981] 1 All ER 303 g. However, Lord Edmund-Davies "found it irksome that the appeal had been conducted on the basis that . . . it [was] beyond doubt that the court would have been justified in dismissing the action on the ground that the plaintiff's inordinate and inexcusable delay had rendered a fair trial impossible," [1981] 1 All ER 302 j. Lord Diplock stated: "If it [the arbitration agreement] creates any contractual obligation to proceed with reasonable dispatch [and he decided that it did] . . . the obligation is, in my view, mutual: it obliges each party to co-operate with the other in taking appropriate steps to keep the procedure in the arbitration moving, whether he happens to be the claimant or the respondent in the particular dispute," [1981] 1 All ER 299 h. Diplock was supported by Lord Edmund-Davies and Lord Russell of Killowen; and opposed by Lord Fraser of Tullybelton and Lord Scarman. Following a detailed observation on the above case and many other cases by The Rt. Hon. Lord Justice Bingham, in giving *THE FRESHFIELDS ARBITRATION LECTURE 1989*, "The Problem of Delay in Arbitration," an attempt was made to resolve the issue in The Courts and Legal Services Act 1990, in section 102. But the effect of this new provision may not be known for some considerable time. [N.B. a very recent case has demolished the "Diplock" concept. Lord Mustill, in *L'Office Cherifien des Phosphates v. Yamashita-Shinnihon Steamship Co Ltd, The Boucraa*, [1994] 1 All ER 20 at

p. 33,c, said: "Freed from the shackles of that [Diplock's] doctrine the arbitrator is to be at liberty to consider whether, in terms of practicalities rather than theories, the delay was the claimant's fault. If the claimant puts up excuses, and the arbitrator rejects them, the delay must be inexcusable within the intendment of Parliament." He said also, "This regime [section 13A of the Arbitration Act 1950] knows nothing of mutual obligations to apply to the court for orders that the plaintiff shall proceed. The onus is firmly on the plaintiff to make things happen without the need for an order and without the need for prompting by the defendant." However, I take the view that Lord Diplock was probably more right than wrong for arbitration, whereas Mustill is right for litigation, but more wrong than right for arbitration. On a detailed anyalsis, the "Diplock" concept may have been wrong in identifying the mutual obligation as being between the parties. I believe the true mutuality is that the parties jointly have an obligation to the arbitrator to do all within their power to bring the arbitration to a conclusion. That mutual obligation would be compatible with the duty placed upon the abritrator to determine the dispute by an award within a reasonable time.

26. The reference to this issue being a "core problem" is certainly not an overstatement of the situation. No one with any sense would recommend that anyone should enter into a contract about which they know nothing. Yet with arbitration agreements that is - in effect - precisely what the recommendation seems to be; at least, each time the arbitration agreement is placed within a standard form of contract.

27. It would be easy to fill a complete book with quotations expressing complaints about arbitration. I don't wish to do that. Instead, I refer to what appears to be a conservative observation by Professor John Uff, Q.C.: "This paper addresses the questions of efficiency and cost-effectiveness in arbitration. There have been many calls for better procedures to be developed, but few constructive proposals." ("Cost-effective arbitration," *(1993) 59, JCI Arb. 1,* p. 39). Underlying Uff's observations are all the concerns that plague arbitration; at least concerns as perceived by those who may rightly claim to have more knowledge than most about this private procedure of dispute resolution.

28. It must be right to say that most people would be reluctant to take part in any form of dispute resolution procedure and would do so only in the absence of some better course; like a negotiated settlement of any problems. In the natural order of things, the least reluctance would be for some form of conciliation, then arbitration, then litigation. The problem seems to be that people in dispute are unsure about arbitration being a procedure to be chosen as the "sensible compromise" between conciliation and litigation. Disputants are said to be hard pressed to decide which of arbitration and litigation is the better, or worse.

29. Section 32 of the Arbitration Act 1950, refers to "arbitration agreement." Such an agreement can only properly come about by consent. *Osborn's Concise Law Dictionary* describes "agreement" in the following terms: "The concurrence of two or more persons in affecting or altering their rights and duties. An agreement is an act in the law whereby two or more persons declare their consent as to any act or thing to be done or forborne by some or one of those persons for the benefit of the others or other of them." It is also clear that an arbitration

agreement is collateral or ancillary to the principal contract, unless expressly stated to be independent of any particular contract.

30. Arbitration is a private matter and thus there is very little evidence as to the conduct of the procedure in times long since past. Even today, there is no real evidence unless the procedure of a particular dispute is tested in the courts. There is, of course, the testimony of those involved in arbitrations in recent times but there is no testimony to show that what has been stated in the text is not true. Moreover, human nature tells us that it is true.

31. See 16.

32. The first Arbitration Act was in 1698, an amendment came in 1835, another amendment in 1854, then the major Act of 1889 which along with the 1934 Act was consolidated into the Arbitration Act 1950.

33. Many references by way of quotations from the continuing debate about arbitration and a potential new Arbitration Bill could be provided to support the comment, and by way of example, see: "Towards a New Arbitration Act," by The Rt. Hon. Lord Justice Steyn, *(1982) 58, JCI Arb. 2,* p. 79. But a particularly pertinent reference is an observation by Lord Hacking, who was said by many to have kicked the ball into play for the Arbitration Act 1979 (see his speech to the House of Lords, "International Arbitration London," *HANSARD,* 15th May 1978, col. 89). Lord Hacking stated: "If our Arbitration Act of 1979 did nothing else, it concentrated attention on the state of our arbitration law." ("Where we are now: a review of English Arbitration Law in the wake of the Arbitration Act 1979," *ARBITRATION,* February 1986, p. 17).

34. Section 27 of the Arbitration Act 1889, states: "'Submission' means a written agreement to submit present or future differences to arbitration, whether an arbitrator is named therein or not." The Arbitration Act 1934, in s. 21(2) changed the word 'submission' to 'arbitration agreement'; and with that amendment the same wording appeared in s. 32 of the Arbitration Act 1950, which remains current at the date of this publication.

35. All that would be necessary is a simple agreement which states something like this: "We the undersigned agree to submit our dispute about . . . to arbitration." No more is necessary, even a simple exchange of letters will do. It is not even necessary to identify the actual topic of the dispute as long as the parties are clearly identified.

36. See 150.

37. The list would be endless, ranging from British Telecom's terms to complicated building and civil engineering and shipping contracts. From leases for commercial property to terms for holiday travel. There are so many. Indeed, it may be the case that the absence of an arbitration agreement in a standard form would be the exception.

38. The Chartered Institute of Arbitrators produce brochures to hand out to people who may be interested in arbitration. As would be expected these stress the benefits of arbitration.

39. On the 6th February 1979, the Institute of Arbitrators was granted a Royal Charter. The first stated object for which the Institute was established is this: "To promote and facilitate the determination of disputes by arbitration."

40. A specific statement incorporated within the Law Society's "Guide to the Professional Conduct of Solicitors," would serve the purpose. Since 1989, when direct professional access to barristers was made possible, it may be necessary for an equivalent statement to be incorporated within The Bar's Code of Conduct.

41. See 14. Mustill & Boyd express the view that, "It is sufficient for the clause to be incorporated by reference either to a standard form of clause or to a set of trade terms which themselves include provisions requiring disputes to be submitted to arbitration." (their second edition), p. 105. However, the case of *Aughton Ltd v. M.F. Kent Services Ltd*, BLR 57, p. 6, sets out a contrary position. Clarity is always better than inferences after the event.

42. See 25.

43. See page 74.

44. See page 27.

45. Section 5 of the Arbitration Act 1979 is all about delays, primarily by the respondent, although it does not specifically say that. And the new provision, section 13A of the Arbitration Act 1950 (brought in by section 102 of the Courts and Legal Services Act 1990) is all about delays by the claimant. These provisions were made necessary because of the problems of reluctancy.

46. Lord Denning, when commencing his judgment in the Appeal Court decision on the *Bremer Vulcan* case ([1980] 1 All ER 425) related the old story which he often told, namely: "When I was young, a sandwich-man wearing a top-hat used to parade outside these courts with his boards back and front, proclaiming 'Arbitrate, don't litigate'." When that story is told, one is often left with the impression that the sandwich-man was involved in some voluntary crusade bent upon converting disputants to resolve their disputes by arbitration. I do not know what the truth is, but I suspect that most sandwich-men are paid to do their job of advertising some product or notion by its promoters. Now, it may well be the case that Lord Denning's sandwich-man was paid by an eager group of arbitrators anxious to promote their own business interests. In which case, the message on the board should have been viewed with the same caution as a message like, "Joe's cafe serves the best food." The real point is this: that most people who promote arbitration, do so in the hope of earning some fees. Or they are paid a salary to promote arbitration, like the staff of the Chartered Institute of Arbitrators. I do not deny that there is always likely to be some people who promote arbitration solely because they believe that it is better for parties in dispute. *[An observer of the "Sandwich*

Man" believed he did the task following an unsuccessful litigation over £1m alleged due to him in connection with the estate of a deceased person.] But, such crusaders should find out about the circumstances of the parties and their dispute before relaying the message; but, for practical purposes that's impossible. I would not like to search for the line between those who promote arbitration for personal gain and those who are totally altruistic in seeking to help others in plight arising out of a dispute. But I do believe that we must all recognise that in many cases the only people who would suffer, in the event that parties in dispute turned away from arbitration, would be the potential arbitrator and possibly the experts too.

47. I do not believe anyone could gainsay that a choice based on knowledge is far superior to one based on ignorance. The problem has always been about how the knowledge can be implanted into the heads of the people concerned prior to their making the choice.

48. There are many members of the Chartered Institute of Arbitrators who will remember the anecdotes told by Norman Royce when explaining how he dealt with some arbitrations. I do not intend to list any of the anecdotes, although they would make for good reading. However, Royce's own words sum up the situation precisely, he said, "Over the years arbitration has changed from a genial occupation to a quite complicated pursuit." ("The 1990 Bill Tompkins Memorial Lecture," *(1991) 57 JCI Arb. 2*, p. 108.) Perhaps the change arose as Royce firstly dealt with arbitrations of a smaller nature where parties represented themselves and then, in due course, his services were required for large arbitrations where the parties were represented by lawyers.

49. The Consumer Arbitration Agreements Act 1988. It applies to England, Wales and Northern Ireland and also includes a section applicable to Scotland. It is a brief Act consisting of only a few sections. The text of the dialogue in this book covers the main purpose of the Act.

50. From my own experience, I have found that many, if not most, people in business are quite ignorant of matters concerning law generally and specifically the contracts into which they have entered. Indeed, this is not surprising because even many lawyers are not fully aware of areas of the law in which they do not specialise. And, in any event, the more one specialises the less one knows about other things, so the business man who specialises in the specific work of his business is likely to be vulnerable in most areas outside that specialisation. The greatest difficulty for all is being aware of what one does not know. It is safer to accept that one knows nothing about anything other than one's field of specialisation. The real danger is when one knows too little about one's own area of specialisation and only a little about other things. The more one studies the more one has to face that problem. It is thus wiser to accept the general inadequacy of knowledge possessed by people, than to do the reverse.

51. In order for the dispute to fall within the time-limits for litigation, there would need to be an amendment to the limitation periods to ensure that the date of notice of arbitration became the effective date for instigation of litigation. Although it is the case that the proposition anticipates that a speedy decision not to proceed with arbitration may be the outcome of "the

pause" for reflection, it may well be the case that the original notice of arbitration may not have been given until almost the expiry of any limitation period.

52. It is difficult to draw comparisons about the merits of each type of dispute procedure. The merits or otherwise depend solely upon the circumstances of the actual dispute. It is, thus, essential that all aspects about a dispute, including the particular circumstances of the parties, are understood before the procedure for resolution is decided upon. In litigation, that option to decide is up to the plaintiff, in all other forms of dispute resolution, the choice is by agreement. The real problem with arbitration is that the agreement is often made prior to a dispute arising and that means the potential for choosing arbitration incorrectly is highly possible. But of significant importance is this: that disputing parties often believe that the choice was wrong because they have no knowledge of the alternatives and no option to explore their greater suitability because they are bound to arbitration.

53. The author's booklet, *ARBITRATION: Recommendations & Survey*, (Herne Bay: Ruthtrek Limited, 1988), ISBN 0 9514295 0 7, see p.11.

54. I do not expect that the proposal for "a pause" will be readily accepted as a solution by the professional and trade bodies. However, there needs to be something better than the usual provisions for arbitration. There needs to be an arrangement which ensures a choice of arbitration based on knowledge.

55. The arrangements for such "a pause" would need to be subject to a time-limit and to an alternative choice being made within the time-limit. But, it must never be forgotten that the parties do always have the power to agree whatever they wish on all issues that are pertinent to them alone. Nevertheless, the arrangement would need to be more than simply "an agreement to agree," (viz. *Courtney and Fairbairn Limited v. Tolaini Brothers (Hotels) Limited*, [1975] 1 All ER 716) in order to ensure the appointment of an arbitrator in the first place.

56. Mustill & Boyd confirm that the relationship "is largely unchartered except as regards certain principles applying to the arbitrator remuneration." (Their second edition, p. 220.) Further, Bernstein & Wood state that, "An arbitrator is . . . appointed in pursuance of a contract. . . . Whether the appointment itself creates a second contract, namely a contract between him and the parties to the arbitration agreement, is a matter of considerable doubt." (*Handbook of Arbitration Practice*, second edition, 1993, p. 44.) Thus, one can say that without clarity of the relationship between the arbitrator and the parties, there is little understanding about the true nature of anything which brings an arbitration into being.

57. An arbitration agreement would seem to lack much of the criteria for a normal agreement. For example, there would be insurmountable problems for the parties to incorporate Liquidated and Ascertained damages for any failure by either party. First, there would be difficulty in showing that the damages were the product of a genuine pre-estimate of the consequences of likely events. Secondly, if the damages were to be a genuine pre-estimate, they would most likely be quite different sums for each of the parties. Moreover, such a provision

would fly in the face of s. 18 of the Arbitration Act 1950, which identifies the manner in which costs shall be awarded. The purpose of this observation is simply to assist in diverting any thoughts away from the notion of an arbitration agreement being akin to a simple contract.

58. "Penalise" is always the wrong word but everyone knows what it means. If a party wishes to amend his pleadings, then an arbitrator may well high-light the factor of "costs" which may be involved before giving consent for the amendment; hence the party may be, in effect, penalised for a failure to get his pleading right in the first place. See also 59.

59. In 1978, Lord Donaldson (then Donaldson J.) had this to say: "that while the rule that costs should follow the event . . . is the usual rule, it may only be a starting point. It is subject to modification or even to complete reversal if a party has conducted itself or the reference unreasonably." *Tramountana v. Atlantic Shipping* [1978] 2 All ER 879, h.

60. Ex parte: "An application in a judicial proceeding made by one party in the absence of the other." Per Osborn's Concise Law Dictionary.

61. There is a danger in looking upon an arbitrator as an expert in the field of dispute. I doubt that arbitrators can ever be truly considered experts on all the matters before them. If the arbitrator were to be an expert in "defects in decorative materials" then he may not be expert on anything else brought before him in a particular arbitration concerning a dispute caused by a claim that there were "defects in decorative materials." For example his expertise may not extend to the effects of consequent delays in the completion of a building. It seems to me that essentially the arbitrator should be able to understand what the parties have to tell him and also have the ability to choose between their contentions.

62. *Osborn's Concise Law Dictionary*. "A fact is said to be proved when the court is satisfied as to its truth, and the evidence by which that result is produced is called the proof. The general rule is that the burden of proof lies on the party who asserts the affirmative of the issue or question in dispute. When that party adduces evidence sufficient to raise a presumption that what he asserts is true, he is said to shift the burden of proof: that is, his allegation is presumed to be true, unless his opponent adduces evidence to rebut the presumption." Hence decided upon the preponderance of probability.

63. *Halsbury's Law*, Arbitration, para. 713: "An award on an arbitration agreement may, by leave of the High Court or a judge thereof, be enforced in the same manner as a judgment or order to the same effect, and where leave is so given, judgment may be entered in terms of the award. This remedy is only available to a successful party where the award arises out of a written arbitration agreement." (Arbitration Act 1950, sections 26 & 32.) With the higher limits of cases being dealt with by the County Court, many arbitrations awards could now be registered with leave of the County Court.

64. It is a characteristic of dispute resolution that the parties argue about issues from different planes of thinking. It seems also to be the case that such different planes of thinking prevent us

from getting to grips with the fundamentals of the dispute resolution procedure. The observations quoted in the text are expressive of the type of discussion sometimes heard.

65. See also 57.

66. Dr. Albert Jan van den berg observed: "That England badly needs a single statutory code for arbitration [it is extremely difficult for a foreigner to find out which is the actual status of English arbitration law. . . .]." See F.E. Miller's *Precis of the Responses* to Mr. Geoffrey King's address as Chairman of the Chartered Institute of Arbitrators on the 7th June 1988, published March 1989, p. 43/C, which is available from the library of the Chartered Institute of Arbitrators. Some four years later, van den berg repeated the observation in his Freshfield Lecture: ". . . please do change your Arbitration Act(s) so that foreigners will be able to understand them." These words were the quintessence of his concluding remarks. See *(1992) 58, JCI Arb. 4*, p. 274. Van den berg's observations are no less pertinent to the indigenous population. The danger for the indigenous population is that they may believe they know about arbitration and therefore do not research it. Whereas, the foreigner starts off on the assumption that he knows nothing and must search for the information. All researchers will find the inadequacy in the presentation of the laws that govern the arbitration procedure.

67. See 56.

68. Private arbitration pursuant to an arbitration agreement should not be compared with County Court arbitrations. Although small claims arbitrations in the County Court are also held in private, the procedure is standard for all cases and the procedure is fully explained in simple booklets. And, of course, the procedure is commenced unilaterally.

69. *Osborn's Concise law Dictionary*: "A valuable consideration in the sense of law may consist either in some right, interest, profit or benefit accruing to one party, or some forbearance, detriment loss or responsibility given, suffered or undertaken by the other."

70. For consideration to be present in an agreement to arbitrate, the actual consideration must be known at the time of making the agreement. Whatever consideration there may be must be very tenuous at the time of making the agreement. I have no knowledge of anyone identifying that an arbitration agreement is a contract based on consideration. However, Mustill & Boyd state that, "strict compliance with the doctrine of consideration is no longer essential to the existence of a contract, if the circumstances are such as to show that a legally enforceable contract is what the parties really intended." However, they also state that, "If there is a contract between the arbitrator and the parties, it must be of a most unusual kind." See, *The Law and Practice of Commercial Arbitration in England*, (2nd Edition), p. 221.

71. See 9 and 34.

72. See 69 and 70.

73. As in the sense of forbearance.

74. The courts cannot override a contract, they - on the application of a party (the plaintiff) - decide whatever issue is brought before them. Whereas, with an arbitration agreement, the courts maintain a residual power over the whole matter. The residual powers are not defined in any absolute sense, but they exist. For example, there is a residual power under section 4(1) of the Arbitration Act 1950. "Scott v. Avery" type clauses merely defer the residual power. See also 76.

75. See 76.

76. Section 4(1) of the Arbitration Act 1950, states: "[Staying court proceedings where there is submission to arbitration] If any party to an arbitration agreement, or any person claiming through or under him, commences any legal proceedings in any court against any other party to the agreement, or any person claiming through or under him, in respect of any matter agreed to be referred, any party to those legal proceedings may at any time after appearance, and before delivering any pleadings or taking any other steps in the proceedings, apply to that court to stay the proceedings, and that court or a judge thereof, if satisfied that there is no sufficient reason why the matter should not be referred in accordance with the agreement, and that the applicant was, at the time when the proceedings were commenced, and still remains, ready and willing to do all things necessary to the proper conduct of the arbitration, may make an order staying the proceedings."

77. See 25.

78. Generally the commitment is set out in s. 12(1), see 86.

79. The Law Commission in considering fiduciary duties referred back to the old case of, *Welles v. Middleton,* (1784) 1 Cox 112 124-5 where they say that Lord Chancellor Thurlow's judgment included the concept of fiduciary as necessary for the "preservation of mankind." What the Lord Chancellor Thurlow actually stated was this: "There are many instances where this court is obliged to act for the preservation of mankind." The case was about fraud and fiduciary duties. [See *Fiduciary duties and regulatory rules: a consultation paper,* The Law Commission 1992.] The fiduciary concept is apt for the agreement to arbitrate and particularly so for the arbitrator. See Paul Finn's paper where he concluded, "[Fiduciary law] abhors the secret, the undisclosed, the covert personal interest, conflicting duty, etc." [and also] "One vital role we have attributed historically to fiduciary law is that of helping to maintain public confidence in persons and institutions rendering client services to which we attribute particular social importance." *Commercial Aspects of Trusts and Fiduciary Obligations,* (Oxford: Clarendon Press, 1992) p. 41.

80. ". . . arbitration as the final default procedure." But, of course, subject to any rights of appeal to the courts as set out in s. 1 of the Arbitration Act 1979 or any reference to the court in respect of the removal of the arbitrator of misconduct as s. 23 of the Arbitration Act 1950, etc.

81. There is a tendency for those who speak or write on the subject of arbitration to express a view on the various topics and having expressed the view, acknowledge that it is not a universally held view. Nevertheless, they maintain that their view is either correct or admissible. For example, on the big issue of inquisitorial versus adversarial one leading lawyer stated the following: "I do not believe that arbitrators, absent agreement, whether expressed or implied, are bound to follow adversarial procedures. This may be a minority view but it has been said on the highest authority, that the arbitrator is master of his own procedure." (see Arthur L. Marriott, *(1993) 59,JCI Arb. 1*, p. 50). Marriott was, of course, basing his view on the observations of Lord Diplock in the *Bremer Vulcan* case [see 25.]. But what value is such a comment when The Rt. Hon. Lord Justice Steyn, also relying for support upon the *Bremer Vulcan* case states: ". . . in practice the rule emerged that in the absence of express or implied agreement to the contrary, an arbitral tribunal must adopt an adversarial as opposed to inquisitorial procedure." *(1992) 58, JCI Arb. 2*, p. 82.). [N.B. But, note a change in Steyn's view as expressed in his *FRESHFIELDS ARBITRATION LECTURE 1993*. See: Lord Justice Steyn, "England's response to the Model Law of Arbitration," *British Insurance Law Association Journal*, January 1994- No. 84, p.15.] Ordinary people involved in the business of arbitration are entitled to a definitive statement on such issues. And, if there is no definitive statement available from the judiciary or the legislature, then the grey area must be tested in wide debate.

82. See 79.

83. *Osborn's Concise Law Dictionary*: "In general, it is the duty of the party whose legal rights have been infringed to act reasonably in mitigation of damages.

84. For the "Diplock" concept, see 25.

85. For s. 4(1), see 76.

86. S.12(1) of the Arbitration Act 1950 states: "[Conduct of proceedings, witnesses, etc.] Unless a contrary intention is expressed therein, every arbitration agreement shall, where such a provision is applicable to the reference, be deemed to contain a provision that the parties to the reference, and all persons claiming through or under them respectively, shall, subject to any legal objection, submit to be examined by the arbitrator or umpire, on oath or affirmation, in relation to the matters in dispute, and shall, subject as aforesaid, produce before the arbitrator or umpire all documents within their possession or power respectively which may be required or called for, and do all other things which during the proceedings on the reference the arbitrator or umpire may require."

87. There is no doubt in my mind that the genuine party will always suffer in arbitration when faced with an opposing party who is determined to wreck the procedure. And, yet it is the genuine party who seems to believe that he should stick by the arbitration procedure. Let me pose this point: That if a potential claimant believes the potential respondent is likely to be uncooperative in a pending arbitration, then, he should issue a writ in respect of the issues in

dispute. So that the opposing party will have to convince a judge under an application to stay proceedings (s. 4(1) see, 76.) that he is ready and willing to proceed with the arbitration. And, if the opposing party is able to obtain a stay, then it will be much easier to get the arbitrator to act in a robust manner, i.e. because the respondent promised the Court "to do all things necessary to the proper conduct of the arbitration." This, of course, is not a recommendation, it is merely a statement to identify the point about the vulnerability of the genuine party opposed by an obstructive one.

88. S. 18(3) of the Arbitration Act 1950, states: "[Costs] Any provision in an arbitration agreement to the effect that the parties or any party thereto shall in any event pay their or his own costs of the reference or award or any part thereof shall be void." Although I have not found a suitable definitive reference [not even from the Law Society] there seems to be a view that everyone is entitled to be represented by a lawyer should that be their wish and that right cannot be excluded by prior agreement.

89. It is obvious that the masses do not require conversion, how could they, when they would not have any existing concept to be converted from? The masses require knowledge, but that is an impossible undertaking. The "masses" is used loosely to cover those people, knowledgeable about arbitration, who take a different view to that expressed.

90. For ADR, see 12.

91. See 98 and 190.

92. See 79.

93. No. That is not quite correct. S. 29 is only about an amendment to the wording of s. 496(3) of the Merchant Shipping Act, 1894. Section 496(3) uses the term "legal proceedings" and section 29 says that "legal proceedings" shall include arbitration and, thus, a definitive commencement date had to be set out. Hence the definition in s. 29(2). It is important to look to the arbitration agreement to discover how the arbitration will commence. If the arbitration agreement is silent about commencement then the mode of commencement, as between the parties, will be implied. It is likely, in the absence of any other relevant criteria, that the courts would imply wording very much on the same lines as s. 29(2), but that is not in itself definitive. Section 29(2) of the Arbitration Act 1950, states: ". . . an arbitration shall be deemed to be commenced when one party to the arbitration agreement serves on the other party or parties a notice requiring him or them to appoint or concur in appointing an arbitrator, or, where the arbitration agreement provides that the reference shall be to a person named or designated in the agreement, requiring him or them to submit the dispute to the person so named or designated." But, that notice can only be given once it is established that a dispute has arisen. When dealing with the question of "Limitation by Statute" one must look to s. 34(1) of the Limitations Act 1980.

94. See page 22; where discussion about "a pause" starts, viz. "S... It may well be the case. . . ."

95. See 76. But, this is strategy and not true procedural issues, i.e., manipulating the procedure to achieve the desired result of an arbitration.

96. See 25.

97. As Lord Donaldson explained, "What is needed now is the creation of a new body of volunteer 'civil justices.' Their task, as a matter of public duty, would be to take their turn in resolving small civil claims, sitting as arbitrators." *(1990) 56, JCI Arb. 1*, p. 15.

98. See the author's article, "Terms of engagement," *The New Law Journal*, 29th November 1991, p. 1633, which reviews the problems of accepting an appointment as arbitrator and settling terms of engagement of the arbitrator.

99. It is simpler merely to refer to "arbitrator" than to all the variety of tribunals but, it is necessary to make clear that all tribunals formed under an arbitration agreement are intended to be in mind.

100. See 113.

101. See 66.

102. Mustill & Boyd, *Commercial Arbitration*, (London: Butterworth, 1982), pp. xxxix - lxxiv.

103. See 66.

104. The Commercial Court Committee, *Report on Arbitration*, Cmnd. 7284, July 1978, noted the demand of consortia which include foreign governments and their agencies who seek to have their disputes settled by arbitration under English Law, but who were deterred by the case stated procedure. However, many of the names of cases before the courts seem to imply that much of the appeals to the courts arose out of these foreign cases. For example, Lord Diplock said, in the case of, *Bremer Vulcan v South India Shipping*, [1981] 1 All ER, p. 292, "The only connection that the whole transaction had with England was that the contract contained an arbitration clause couched in the widest terms providing that any dispute or difference shall be referred to Arbitration in London within the meaning of the English Arbitration Act 1950, and the rules, regulations, etc., of the said Act shall solely apply." There is no doubt that the *Bremer Vulcan* case turned the law upside down. The other case which turned it around again also had a foreign sounding name: *L'Office Cherifien des Phosphates v. Yamashita-Shinnihon Steamship Co Ltd, The Boucraa*, [1994] 1 All ER 20, see 25.

105. See 104. See also article by Adrian Jack, "Civil Justice Review," *Counsel*, May/June 1994, p. 15, where he stated; "yet the Commercial Court is largely used by foreigners with no particular connection with the United Kingdom."

106. ". . . relatively minor sums," is used in the context of the costs of taking an action through the whole procedure leading to a House of Lords' decision.

107. See *Harbutt's Plasticine Ltd V Wayne Tank and Pump Co Ltd*, [1970] 1 All ER 225, overruled by *Photo Production Ltd v. Securicor Transport Ltd* [1980] 1 All ER 556.

108. See Partick Devlin, Lord, *The Judge*, p. 107, and the subsequent support given to the theme of allowing the *ex aequo et bono* into arbitration by Stewart Boyd Q.C. See the latter's paper, "Arbitrator not to be bound by the Law" Clauses, *The Ronald Bernstein Lectures 1989*. See also 5(a).

109. See 79.

110. Of course, this would be simply a manipulation of the system. But, in some respects, it is not too dissimilar to the result when a large insurance company or the government select a test-case for the courts; and the other party is a mere member of the public without all the necessary resources.

111. See 98.

112. See 66.

113. There is no doubt that the actions of the parties would, in part, fashion the nature of the implied terms, but generally terms can only be implied because they are so obvious from the context of the arrangements made by the parties or implied because they are normal terms relative to the type of arrangement entered into by the parties. "An implied warranty . . . as distinguished from an express contract or express warranty, really is in every instance founded upon the presumed intention of the parties and upon reason." per Bowen L.J., *The Moorcock*

114. See 113. See also the author's article, "Arbitration: negligence and the arbitrator," *Professional Negligence*, vol. 9, No. 2, 1993, p. 72, where it was suggested "that the Judge's remarks in *Pratt v. Swanmore Builders Limited*, were subjective rather than objective."

115. See 98.

116. There is nothing to challenge the reasoning set down in the text.

117. See the author's booklet, *ARBITRATION: Recommendations & Survey*, for significant evidence about the admission to lack of knowledge by many of those who claim to have an interest in arbitration, by virtue of their membership of the Chartered Institute of Arbitrators.

118. See the author's article, "Redefining terms of arbitration," *The New Law Journal*, 8th June 1990, p. 827.

119. See 118.

120. For example: Mustill & Boyd's, *Commercial Arbitration* and Bernstein & Wood's *Handbook of Arbitration Practice*, to name but two of the many books available.

121. The text identifies the obvious outcome of the flexibility afforded by lack of a definition and the rigidity if there were a definition. See 122.

122. Following my research, I concluded that either the term, "arbitration" must be defined or it must be treated as a *word of art* [see my article referred to in 118.]. Only the latter would give the flexibility to enable anyone to use arbitration. The former would push arbitration more towards the concepts of litigation. Unless, of course, one had a definition that was so wide that on analysis the defined procedure probably could not be defined as "arbitration."

123. Arbitration Act 1698 (9 & 10 Will. III c. 15) states:

"Whereas it hath been found by experience, that references made by rule of Court have contributed much to the ease of the subject, in the determining of controversies, because the parties become thereby obliged to submit to the award of the arbitrators, under the penalty of imprisonment for their contempt in case they refuse submission;

"Now for promoting trade and rendering the awards of arbitrators the more effectual in all cases, for the final determination of controversies referred to them by merchants and traders or others, concerning matters of account or trade, or other matters; [the Act then sets out the provisions]"

124. See 98. and 125.

125. *The K/S Norjarl A/S v Hyundai Heavy Industries Co Ltd* [1991] 1 Lloyd's Report 268, is evidence of the "mix up." Mr Justice Phillips stated, "As this case demonstrates, it is highly desirable that any negotiations between the arbitrators and the parties as to the services that the arbitrators are to render and the terms upon which they are to render them should take place at the time of the appointment of the arbitrators." In this case, there was no complete common ground between all three members of the tribunal and the parties about the terms of the engagement of the tribunal, thus inevitably there were implanted the destructive spores which developed into an issue which was left to be resolved by the Court of Appeal.

126. See 98.

127. For example: the various rules of the Chartered Institute of Arbitrator, which range from those dealing with the small consumer schemes to those dealing with large commercial disputes.

128. On one side there are the potentially complex disputes over matters like double glazing, where often a site visit is necessary, and much time can be spent on one dispute. On the other hand there are the disputes over British Telecom charges or compensations which are inevitably all office bound activities.

129. See interesting article by Bruce Harris, "Procedural Problems in Arbitration," *(1991) 57, JCI Arb. 2*, p. 83.

130. For example: *the Society of Construction Arbitrators*, "Form of agreement for the appointment of an arbitrator."

131. "The London Bar Arbitration Scheme," is promoted by the London Common Law and Commercial Bar Association, 3 Gray's Inn Place, London, WC1R 5EA, Edition March 1992. But note, that an exclusion for liability is kept separate from the, "Terms of Appointment," see para. 7, p. 12.

132. For example: the Chartered Institute of Arbitrators' "Arbitration Rules," 1988 Edition, available from the International Arbitration Centre, 24 Angel Gate, City Road, London, EC1V 2RS.

133. The draft Arbitration Bill as set out in the Department of Trade and Industry's *A Consultation Paper on Draft Clauses and Schedules of an Arbitration Bill*, February 1994, includes immunity in this form: "Neither an arbitrator nor an umpire, nor any servant of an arbitrator or umpire, shall be liable in damages for anything done or omitted in the discharge or purported discharge of his functions as arbitrator or umpire unless the act or omission is shown to have been taken in bad faith." To some readers this may sound like good news but the Departmental Advisory Committee simply "recommended that a provision should be included in the draft Bill in order to focus attention on the issue for the purpose of consultation." (see note 10 Part III, 13). However, I take the view that the end result of this action by the DAC will result in the provision being dropped in order to avoid anything of a controversial nature preventing the new Bill going through smoothly. And, that would have the same effect as saying that arbitrators do not have such immunity. It would be difficult to argue the opposing case if the provision were dropped.

134. See 98.See also 131, where the London Bar Association Scheme seeks to achieve this ideal.

135. In effect, the *Rules of the Supreme Court* would need to include a set of terms of engagement based upon which the Court will appoint an arbitrator. Such terms are likely to be different from those produced by a professional or trade body. However, I believe that such a step by the Court would probably solve everyone's problem because the terms used by the court could be the default terms for everyone.

136. The draft Arbitration Bill as set out in the Department of Trade and Industry's *A Consultation Paper on Draft Clauses and Schedules of an Arbitration Bill*, February 1994, (see

note 10, Part III, p. 12), shows quite clearly that the problem is known about. It is also clear that there is much opposition to the notion of arbitrators having judicial immunity, some would certainly prefer that they dealt with the issue by way of Professional Indemnity, q.v. 192.

137. I have researched the big issues of Third Parties & Consolidation and of Inquisitorial & Adversarial procedures. [See The author's booklet, *ARBITRATION: Recommendations & Survey.*] It is quite clear that the issues should be debated until a conclusion is reached. The simple statement of one view and another identifies the uncertainty that needs to be resolved but - as is mostly the case with arbitration - the issues are not resolved, they are merely high-lighted as a problem.

138. See Appendix p. 115.

139. There is a tendency, especially in government contracts, to identify all clauses in a contract as being conditions. For example: see GC/Works/1 series. The idea is no doubt to convey the impression that the breach of any terms will go to the root of the contract.

140. See Appendix p. 115.

141. See 98. and 129.

142. My object in writing this book is to encourage wide debate on the topics. The issues should be debated until a conclusion is reached. If the work of this book only makes out the case: that there is a need to resolved the issues considered, then it may have been useful, but it would have failed in its purpose. The issues are capable of resolution and it is the purpose of this book to demand a resolution by way of informed debate.

143. See 93.

144. See Appendix p 115.

145. This aspect about the knowledge possessed by people in organisations dealing with specific matters is too often neglected. In my view, one must regard it to be a bonus if the administrative staff in a specialist body are experts on the subject matter concerning the body. For example, it would be quite wrong to assume that all the employed administrative staff in the Royal Institute of British Architects should be regarded to be as qualified as the members of that professional body. Maybe some are, maybe not. But it is dangerous to assume clerks know more than a minimal level about the technical aspect of the issues involved. Even where the members of the administrative staff may have some special qualification, like being a lawyer, it does not mean that there is any particular understanding on the actual issue in hand. Of what value would anyone's qualification be, if the employed administrative staff in the professional body were all generally as competent in the business of the qualified member ?

146. Checking the validity of the arbitration clause and the appointment is something which every arbitrator should do, but checking is not the same as having the power to decide. However, the arbitrator has the power to decide whether or not there is a dispute, that was made clear by Lord Diplock. See 157.

147. See 66.

148. My studies have led me to consider these issues of uncertainty in the law and brief recommendations were made following those studies. These issues are likely to dominate the debates on litigation over the years ahead, more so than ever before. Advances in Information Technology will ensure that the inadequacies of the courts to deliver clarity are well and truly exposed. This is not, in any way, a criticism of the judiciary as such, it is merely a reflection on the need to recognise that the system within which the judiciary have to operate is not satisfactory; and it's no good pretending that it is. See, Author's booklet, *Arbitration: Recommendations & Survey*, p. 16.

149. At a future time, I will seek to expand upon the recommendations to which I have referred, see 148.

150. See Mustill & Boyd, *Commercial Arbitration* (second edition) p. 41, for a list of the attributes which must be present in an arbitration and also their general discussion of the topic. See also Bernstein & Wood, *The Handbook of Arbitration Practice* (second edition), section 4, pp. 21 - 33.

151. The draft Arbitration Bill as set out in the Department of Trade and Industry's, *A Consultation Paper on Draft Clauses and Schedules of an Arbitration Bill*, February 1994, (see note 4, Part III, pp. 3 - 7,) where the words of Lord Devlin are quoted, namely: "[The arbitrators are entitled, in short, to make their own inquiries in order to determine their own course of action, and the result of that inquiry has no effect whatsoever upon the rights of the parties."] The *Consultation Paper* gives a broad analysis of case law on this topic.

152. This type of issue always forces one to return to the degree of knowledge expected of an arbitrator and the parties. As the law does not expect any of them to have any particular knowledge, any claim founded upon such problems must be subjective and that is not a good foundation for claims of damages for negligence unless there is an express obligation or warranty about knowledge. See also 13 and 114.

153. Perhaps the arbitrator should seek an indemnity from the party or parties seeking his appointment, see text, p. 63.

154. In the recent case of *Palacath Ltd v. Flanagan*, [1985] 2 All ER 165, the judge said that the statement of the judge in *Taylor v. Yielding* (1912) 56 SJ 253 was a very potent matter and must be taken into account. The words referred to were these: "You cannot make a valuer an

arbitrator by calling him so, or vice versa." In other words, what is or is not an arbitration is not based on the choice of the parties but is a matter of law to be decided by the courts.

155. see 152.

156. To explain the words of a contract by using other words must give a different meaning to the words used. Only the courts have a definitive power to express the meaning of a contract in words other than the words actually used, and that they will do generally only to achieve efficacy.

157. See the *Bremer Vulcan* case where Lord Diplock considered the position where "one party claims that no dispute has arisen under [the arbitration agreement]." and he stated, "Whether there is a dispute or not is a matter to be decided by the arbitrator, and no injunction [to restrain proceedings] will be granted. [1981] 1 All ER, 300, see line (a). See Appendix, p. 118.

158. It is really a matter of common sense, if the appointed arbitrator is able to see obvious irregularities he should draw these to the attention of the parties before accepting the appointment, but it is no use trying to decide anything without the benefit of hearing what the parties have to say on the point. And that cannot be done effectively unless the appointed arbitrator accepts the appointment. See also 157.

159. I submitted a copy of my draft conditions to the Chartered Institute of Arbitrators in 1983, see Appendix p. 107, and again raised the matter at the Annual Conference (1988), in Dublin, where my remarks were reported, thus: "Francis Miller . . . asked that, if and when, the [arbitration] rules were again revised, they could be expanded to include a Model Exclusion Agreement and also a Model Form of Conditions of Engagement for Arbitrators." *Arbitration*, Vol. 55, No. 1, February 1989, p. 20.

160. See text p. 118 [adjacent 157.].

161. See Appendix p. 113, para. 1.

162. See Appendix p. 113, para. 2.

163. The circumstances noted are those where the arbitrator refuses to part with his award until his fees are paid. If the arbitrator does part with the award prior to payment, he will have to sue for his money in the normal way, should the parties not pay on demand. See 164. for provisions of the 1950 Act.

164. This point is covered by s. 19 of the Arbitration Act 1950 which states: "[Taxation of arbitrator's or umpire's fees] (1) If in any case an arbitrator or umpire refuses to deliver his award except on payment of the fees demanded by him, the High Court may, on an application for the purpose, order that the arbitrator or umpire shall deliver the award to the applicant on payment into court by the applicant of the fees demanded, and further that the fees demanded

shall be taxed by the taxing officer and that out of the money paid into court there shall be paid out to the arbitrator or umpire by way of fees such sum as may be found reasonable on taxation and that the balance money, if any, shall be paid out to the applicant."

165. See Appendix p. 113, para. 3.

166. This provision does not appear in the Appendix. This, as has been stated, has nothing to do with the arbitrator. Perhaps it would be right to put such a provision in the arbitration agreement, by virtue of the agreement referring to a set of rules which included it, but it should be obvious in any event. Some argue that what seems obvious to the expert is not so obvious to the parties, but even so the topic is outside the concern of the arbitrator and his own conditions of engagement.

167. See Appendix p. 113, para. 5.

168. See the results of research into "Cancellation Charges," by Bruce Harris. *Arbitration*, Vol. 55, No. 1, February 1989, p. 59.

169. Giving written notice is usually an essential part in supporting a subsequent case for recovery of loss and expense, it should be no less the case in arbitration.

170. That is the difficulty with, and the cause of criticism of, model forms containing standard cancellation charges. Like liquidated damages, they too can be moulded into an effective penalty, even though justified by prior calculation; one can do much as one pleases with projections of cost.

171. It seems to be quite wrong that costs can mount up to very high figures without everyone knowing what is at stake. In fact, it seems to be often the case that a party is not fully aware of his own costs as the dispute proceeds, let alone being aware of the costs of the other party and those of the arbitrator.

172. Professor Bernardo Cremades said, "By arbitration the parties are not seeking a solution which is inferior to the judicial settlement; rather they are endeavouring to have their dispute settled in the same contractual atmosphere as they had drawn up and anticipated implementation would take place of the contract, the interpretation whereof has created the dispute now to be settled." See his paper, "Should arbitrators maintain their independence or would it be desirable for them to have closer links with the courts in their respective countries?", *Arbitration*, Vol. 44 No. 2, January 1978, p.85. In whatever way one may relate arbitration to litigation, there is no doubt that the concept of settling a dispute in the same environment as that in which the contract was forged is the essence of arbitration. Those who may be carefree about setting down the terms of their contracts perhaps should be very flexible as to the solution of problems arising out of their prior carefreeness.

173. Professor John Uff said, "The modern arbitrator, however, has to deal with skilled lawyers whose task is to preserve all the rights and interests of their clients, even though this may not be conducive to efficiency or cost effectiveness." See his paper, "cost-effective arbitration," *(1993) 59, JCI Arb. 1*, p.39.

174. Following what apparently turned out to be an onslaught against lawyers, Kerry Harding, the Secretary of the Chartered Institute of Arbitrators, felt obliged to write: "My attention was drawn by a lawyer to the apparently anti-lawyer bias of some of the speakers at the recent very successful Annual Conference in Glasgow." He added that, "Cost-effective arbitration can only be achieved by teamwork between the arbitrator(s) and the representatives - lay or legal - of the parties in dispute." *(1994) 60, JCI Arb. 1*, p. 68.

175. See 12.

176. Anyone who has dealings with the courts will discover how user-friendly the system is becoming. See the customer charters published, especially for lay public dealings with the County Courts.

177. The judges of the Official Referees' Court are "doing the rounds" and telling arbitrators how to handle arbitrations and explaining how they deal with the problems in their own court. For example: His Hon. Judge Bowsher, Q.C.'s address on, "Methods of avoiding delay in arbitration," was very much about, *this is what we do, you should do the same*." See report of his address, *Arbitration - News & Views*, ISSN 0965-5972, Number 18 - July 1992, p. 10.

178. See Appendix p. 113, para. 6.

179. This was the proposal in my article, "Terms of engagement," see 98.

180. Bernstein & Wood in their book, *Handbook of Arbitration Practice*, say this: "It is difficult to envisage a contract of appointment under which the arbitrator has a right to retire at any time and for any reason." (second edition, p. 44) So it is important to recognise the need for some agreement on the matter if the arbitrator is not to be placed at risk.

181. Section 23(2) of the Arbitration Act 1950.

182. See Appendix p. 114, para. 7.

183. This aspect is a problem which should be addressed by the appointing bodies. This was the proposal in my article, "Terms of engagement," see 98. See also 125.

184. Section 19 of the Arbitration Act 1950.

185. See Appendix p. 117.

186. See 98.

187. See Appendix p. 114, para. 8, [same as 185.]

188. See Appendix p. 114, para. 9.

189. A more reasonable concept would be this: that some issues are very complex and it is not easy to find the definitive answer; and naturally there will be divisions on the subject. The alternative to seeing the minority view reported in judgments of the higher courts would be to suppress the minority view; which would be equally unsatisfactory because often it is found later that the minority view is the bold line of thinking which proved correct. But, in any event, the suggestion that there is a deliberate attempt to keep a minority view in focus is likely to be wrong.

190. See the author's article, "Arbitration: negligence and the arbitrator," *Tolley's Professional Negligence*, (1987) 9 PN 70-73, which reviews the uncertainty of the law on this issue. It is the uncertainty of law concerning the arrangement between the arbitrator and the parties which makes acceptance of an arbitration appointment a potential risk for anyone. See also the author's article, "The judicial immunity of arbitrators," *The New Law Journal*, 10th May 1991, p. 633.

191. For details of the survey see questions 3.01 - 3.05 [in particular 3.03], p.20 & 21 and recommendation, p. 8, in the author's booklet, *Arbitration: Recommendations & Survey*.

192. Dugdale & Stanton in their book, *Professional Negligence* said this: "The narrower view [i.e., Lord Kilbrandon's view in the *Arenson* case that there was no justification for arbitrator's judicial immunity] may also be seen as more likely to enhance rather than reduce the quality of arbitral services." (1989 edition, see p. 156) Socrates [so wrote Xenophon] said, ". . . . So a man who did his best to get himself elected to this office without troubling to learn how to discharge it would surely deserve to be penalised."

193. See sections 22 & 23 of the Arbitration Act 1950 and, of course, the powers of review on a point of law; the main purpose of the Arbitration Act 1979. But see also the author's article "Another blunder hits the statute book," *The New Law Journal*, 16th October 1992, p. 1421, where the important case of *The Nema*, [1981] 2 All ER 1030, is high-lighted as a restriction upon the court's discretion.

194. It is obvious that anyone who is asked to advise an arbitrator about whether or not he should protect himself against a claim would have to answer in the affirmative. And, that is precisely what the whole situation is about. In the end, such a situation will be a detriment to arbitration. Perhaps, like other professions, arbitrators will act as limited liability companies. I have heard, in general discussions, barristers state that a limited liability company can act as an arbitrator, but I have never seen such statements in writing. Such a concept seems to be absolute nonsense, but who knows, maybe that will in due course be considered quite normal.

Only a few decades ago, no one would ever have thought about a professional man operating solely behind a limited company. Now it seems to be almost the norm.

195. See author's letter, "Old Po-face," to the editor, *Arbitration*, Vol 49, No. 3, Feb. 1984, p. 266.

196. The issue about the obvious secrecy as between the arbitrator and the parties where the arbitrator is seeking to safeguard his own interest is an aspect of human nature which cannot be ruled out. Ask a policeman "the time" and you expect to be told the truth. Ask him whether he is always truthful when there is an important issued at stake between himself and a "suspect" and you would be unwise to expect a truthful answer, even though you may get one. And that is the problem. The arbitrator would need full immunity from suit so that the parties would know they could accept what he states, because he could then state what he likes without any fear whatsoever. The only concern to face an arbitrator should be public admonishment where justly deserved.

197. See Appendix p. 115.

198. See s. 102 of The Courts and Legal Services Act 1990 [to be inserted as s. 13A of the Arbitration Act 1950] which provides for the arbitrator to dismiss a claim for want of prosecution where there has been inordinate and inexcusable delay. There is a general acceptance that this provision will resolve many of the issues, but I do not believe it will work in reality: see the author's article, "Another blunder hits the statute book," *The New Law Journal*, 16th October 1992, p. 1421. See also Lord Mustill's judgment in *L'Office Cherifien des Phosphates v. Yamashita-Shinnihon Steamship Co Ltd, The Boucraa*, [1994] All ER 20, where he says that the new provision is intended to be retrospective. See also, 25; especially the last three sentences.

199. For details of the survey see question 4.03, p.22 and recommendation, p. 7, in the author's booklet, *Arbitration: Recommendations & Survey.* See also question 6.06, p. 26 and recommendation, p. 11 about where "Arbitration found not suitable," because many problems of delay and frustration in arbitration generally arise from the fact that arbitration is just not suitable for the dispute being decided.

200. See Appendix p. 116.

THE APPENDIX

TEXT USED FOR CRITICISM

The author studied the various "Rules for Arbitration" which had been published at the time (1983) and, using them as a guide, produced the following document; which has been used as the basis of criticism in the text.

[D R A F T]

ARBITRATION RULES

and

CONDITIONS OF ENGAGEMENT

for

DOMESTIC ARBITRATIONS

Prepared by:
Francis E. Miller.

ARBITRATION RESEARCH

February 1983.

NOTE

The parties

These Rules are primarily designed to make the process of arbitration better for the parties involved in a dispute.
None of the Rules are unchangeable; and any may be deleted to suit the parties requirements.

The arbitrator

The conditions of engagement affect the arbitrator's own personal position.
An arbitrator would not be recommeded to accept an appointment without such protection; as is provided by the conditions of engagement.

An arbitrator is generally engaged to determine a matter which the parties have failed to resolve themselves.
And, if the arbitrator is to do his work effectively he needs to know that his own position is secure.

1.00 INTRODUCTION

1.01 These rules and conditions for engagement are recommeded for the use in all arbitrations where a sole arbitrator is appointed by, or on behalf of, the parties to a dispute under an arbitration agreement.

1.02 A separate set of rules and conditions apply in cases where arbitrations are to be administered by the Chartered Institute of Arbitrators.

1.03 These rules and conditions comprise four sections, namely:

2.00 JURISDICTION AND POWERS OF THE ARBITRATOR.

3.00 PROCEDURE OF THE ARBITRATION.

4.00 EXCLUSION AGREEMENT (optional).

5.00 CONDITIONS FOR ENGAGEMENT OF THE ARBITRATOR.

1.04 These rules are intended for application in their entirety and great care should be exercised before making deletions or amendments to suit individual circumstances.

1.05 Where the word "party" is used in these Rules it means a party to the dispute referred to arbitration; and shall also include his representatives.

1.06 A "domestic arbitration agreement" means an agreement defined by section (3)(7) of the Arbitration Act 1979; and, where the law of England is applicable.

2.00 JURISDICTION AND POWERS OF THE ARBITRATOR

Jurisdiction generally

2.01 Insofar as English Law allows, the arbitrator shall be vested with the following general powers in addition to those specifically provided for in the Arbitration Acts of 1950 and 1979:

2.01.01 To determine any question as to the validity, extent or continuation of any contract between the parties.

2.01.02 To order the correction or amendment of any term or condition in any contract between the parties and related to the matter in dispute which the arbitrator determines to have been the common intention of the parties.

2.01.03 To order the correction or amendment of any term or condition in the arbitration agreement, submission or reference which

the arbitrator determines to have been the common intention of the parties.

2.01.04 To determine any question of law arising in the arbitration.

2.01.05 To determine any question as to his own jurisdiction.

2.01.06 To determine any question of good faith, dishonesty or fraud arising out of the dispute.

2.01.07 To order any party to furnish him with such further details of its case, in fact or law, as he may require.

2.01.08 To proceed in the arbitration notwithstanding the failure or refusal of any party to comply with these Rules or with his orders or directions, or to attend any meeting or hearing, but only after giving that party written notice that he intends to do so.

2.01.09 To receive and take into account such written or oral evidence as he shall determine to be relevant. The strict rules of evidence shall not apply.

2.01.10 To make more than one interim award.

2.01.11 To order the parties to make interim payments towards the costs of the arbitration.

2.01.12 To hold meetings and hearings in England and elsewhere.

2.01.13 To express his award in any currency.

2.01.14 To award interest on any sum from and to any date at such rates as he determines to be appropriate.

Special powers

2.02 On acceptance of these Rules by the parties, the arbitrator shall, thereupon, have the following special powers; unless subsequently rescinded by agreement between all the parties to the dispute.

2.03 The arbitrator may of his own motion, or on the application of any of the parties, exercise any of the following powers:

2.03.01 To allow other parties to be joined in the arbitration with their express consent, and make a single final award determining all disputes between them.

2.03.02 To allow any party, upon such terms (as to costs and otherwise) as he shall determine, to amend his Statement of Case, Defence or Reply.

2.03.03 To extend or abbreviate any time limits provided by these Rules or by his directions.

2.03.04 To rely on his own expert knowledge and experience in any field (without obligation to prove the existence of such knowledge or experience), or appoint one or more advisors or experts on any matter (including law) to assist him in the conduct of the arbitration..

2.03.05 To conduct such enquiries as may appear to him to be necessary or expedient.

2.03.06 To order the parties to make any property or thing available for his inspection, and to inspect it in their presence.

2.03.07 To order any party to produce to him any documents in their power and possession in order to determine the relevance of such documents; and to order that copies of documents so determined as relevant be made available to all other parties.

2.03.08 To order the preservation, storage, sale or other disposal of any property or thing under the control of any of the parties.

2.03.09 To make interim orders for security for any party's own cost, and to secure all or part of any amount in dispute in the arbitration.

2.03.10 To determine the time, duration, location and number of meetings and hearings as seems appropriate to deal with the reference.

3.00 **PROCEDURE OF THE ARBITRATION**

3.01 In so far as the Arbitration Acts of 1950 and 1979 allow, and in so far that all the parties to the dispute have not agreed otherwise, the arbitrator shall have absolute discretion as to the procedure of the arbitration.

3.02 The arbitrator shall make known his orders and directions to all the parties.

3.03 Such orders and directions shall be made in writing, or confirmed in writing. And, the parties shall comply with all such orders and direction.

3.04 All communications between the parties and the arbitrator shall be deemed to have been properly delivered if despatched by post, cable, telex or by hand to the addresses as stated in the conditions for engagement of the arbitrator.

3.05 Any party changing his address, or nominating a representative's address, shall give notice in writing to the arbitrator and the other parties of the new address for sevice.

3.06 Any party who makes a written communication to the arbitrator shall forthwith despatch a copy of that

communication to all other parties to the dispute.

3.07 No party shall make an oral communication with the arbitrator except in the presence of, and subject to the awareness of, all other parties.

3.08 With the consent of the parties the arbitrator may, at his sole discretion, decide the dispute on the basis of written statements and documents submitted by the parties. Otherwise, the matter will be heard at a hearing or hearings as appropriate. Such hearing will be held in private and be informal.

3.09 The parties shall give written notice to the arbitrator and to each other of their intention to be represented or assisted by any person, legally qualified or otherwise, either as advocate or expert witness. And, no person other than those covered by such notice will be permitted to take part in any hearing. If, following such written notice, the other party or parties appear to be put at a disadvantage with respect to the time of the hearing the arbitrator may adjourn, or delay, any hearing and take account of the matter when considering costs.

4.00 EXCLUSION AGREEMENT (optional)

THIS AGREEMENT is made
the......day of ....19......
between...
of..
....
and...
of..
....

WHEREAS A DISPUTE has arisen between the above named parties and it has been agreed that all matters in difference between us in respect of the contract dated the......day of..............
19..... would be referred to arbitraton to the award of ....
of..
....

IT IS HEREBY AGREED THAT the parties desire that the dispute shall be determined finally by the said ....
and it is hereby agreed in accordance with section 3 of the Arbitration Act 1979 that the right of appeal by either party to the High Court under section 1 of that Act shall be excluded in relation to the award of the arbitrator on the dispute and that neither party shall have the

- 8 -

right to apply to the High Court under section 2(1)(a) of that Act for the determination of any question of law arising in the course of the reference to arbitration.

For.............................
(Claimants)
Signed on behalf of the above named
in the presence of:-

For.............................
(Respondents)
Signed on behalf of the above named
in the presence of:-

- 9 -

5.00 CONDITIONS OF ENGAGEMENT OF THE ARBITRATOR

WHEREAS a dispute has arisen out of a contract dated the .... of .... 19...... between the undersigned; and

WHEREAS in accordance with the arbitration clause of that contract the parties wish to appoint..
of...
....
..............................to act as sole arbitrator.

[Alternative.
WHEREAS in accordance with the arbitration clause of that contract the.............................
of ....
has appointed ....
of..
....
to act as sole arbitrator.]

The said .... is prepared to act as sole arbitrator on acceptance of the following terms.

1. That the parties shall be jointly and severally liable for the fees and expenses of the arbitrator from the time of appointment to the conclusion of the matter.

2. That the parties shall be jointly and severally liable to take up the award of the arbitrator by payment of the arbitrator's fees and expenses within 14 days of being notified of the amount of such charges and that the award has been published.

3. That if the award is not taken up by the payment of charges, as notified, the arbitrator may, without further notice, proceed against any or all of the parties for recovery of costs, fees and expenses.

4. That if the award has determined that all or any part of the costs of the arbitration shall be paid by any party other than the party which has already paid them, that party shall have the right to recover the appropriate amount from that other party.

5. That if the parties should reach agreement on the matters in dispute, or on termination or abandonment of the dispute before publication of the award, they shall each be under an obligation to forthwith notify the arbitrator of such agreement, and shall be jointly and severally liable to pay the proper charges of the arbitrator as due at that time. Such charges to include any reasonable charges in respect of the cancellation of reserved time and costs in respect of accommodation, etc. which are no longer required.

6. That the arbitrator requires security in the sum of £_______. before proceeding with the reference, and that such security shall, at the determination of the arbitrator, be increased from time to time as the arbitration proceeds. Such

security to be placed in the hands of the Chartered Institute of Arbitrators to hold as stake holder pending submission of interim and final accounts for fees and expenses at any reasonable time within the sole descretion of the arbitrator. The arbitrator shall notify all parties, by copy invoice, of any charges sent to the stake holder.

7. That the arbitrator's fees will be charged at £________. per hour/day in respect of all time spent upon the arbitration and also any travelling time; together with all expenses for travel, subsistence, hire of arbitration rooms, postage, telex, cable, telephone, copying, recording, typing, transcribing, reports of experts and advisors, and any other like items all chargeable at cost. In addition VAT will be added at the appropriate rate.

8. That the arbitrator's fees will be subject to review at six monthly intervals from the date of this agreement.

Exclusion of liability

9. That the arbitrator declines absolutely to accept the risks of having to defend a negligence claim and he shall not be liable for any act or omission in, or in connection with, this arbitration. This absolute exclusion of

liabiltiy extends to all matters except any conscious and deliberate wrongdoing on the part of the arbitrator.

Arbitration Rules (optional)

10. That the arbitrator shall have the jurisdiction and powers set out in sections 1.00, 2.00 and 3.00 of the attached Rules in their printed form; or as amended and initialed by all the parties to this agreement.

For..............................
(Claimants)
Signed on behalf of the above named
in the presence of:-

For..............................
(Respondents)
Signed on behalf of the above named
in the presence of:-

PROPOSED TERMS FOR ENGAGEMENT OF THE ARBITRATOR

NAME AND ADDRESS OF THE ARBITRATOR:

....

....

....

NAME AND ADDRESS OF CLAIMANT:

....

....

....

NAME AND ADDRESS OF RESPONDENT:

....

....

....

THE SUBJECT MATTER OF THE DISPUTE:

....

....

....

....

PARTICULARS OF THE ARBITRATION AGREEMENT AND THE MODE OF THE APPOINTMENT OF AN ARBITRATOR [State how arbitrator is to be appointed]:

....

....

....

....

....

WHEREAS **the Claimant/the Claimant and Respondent has/have** provided security in the sum of £__________ , or will provide such security before seeking the arbitrator to proceed further with the reference and, further, **accepts/accept** that such security shall, at the determination of the arbitrator, be increased from time to time as the arbitration proceeds. And, furthermore, **accepts/accept** that failure to provide adequate security will entitle the arbitrator to refuse to proceed further with the reference and/or to resign. [Such security to be deposited with The Chartered Institute of Arbitrators to hold as stake-holder pending submission of interim and final accounts for fees and expenses at the sole discretion of the arbitrator. The arbitrator shall notify all parties, by way of an invoice charged against the provider of the security, and shall claim release of the appropriate sum from the stake-holder.]

WHEREAS the Claimant and Respondent acknowledge that the arbitrator declines absolutely to accept the risks of having to defend a negligence claim, they agree that he shall not be liable for any act or omission in, or in connection with, this arbitration. [This absolute exclusion of liability shall extend to all matters except any conscious and deliberate wrongdoing on the part of the arbitrator.]

WHEREAS the Claimant and Respondent acknowledge that if the award is not taken up by either party by the payment of fees and expenses, as notified by the arbitrator, the arbitrator may, without further notice, proceed against any or all of the parties for recovery of fees and expenses notified as due.

WHEREAS the Claimant and Respondent acknowledge that the arbitrator whilst being willing and able to do all things reasonably necessary to settle the arbitration by an award he is not prepared to give an open-ended commitment as to time-span. The Claimant and Respondent accept that should the arbitration extend beyond the period of ________ months/ years beyond the date of this appointment, through no fault of the arbitrator, then the arbitrator has the right to review his appointment and, should he so decide, to retire from the appointment without detriment to fees and expenses already due to him.

UPON WRITTEN ACCEPTANCE BY THE ABOVE NAMED PERSON TO UNDERTAKE ALL THE DUTIES OF AN ARBITRATOR TO DETERMINE THE DIFFERENCES BETWEEN THE PARTIES NAMED HEREIN, BOTH THE CLAIMANT AND THE RESPONDENT JOINTLY AND SEVERALLY AGREE TO BE LIABLE IN ACCORDANCE WITH THE FOLLOWING TERMS:-

To be liable for the fees and expenses of the arbitrator from the time of the appointment to the conclusion of the matter.

To be liable to pay the arbitrator's fees at a rate of £_________*# per hour/day in respect of all time reasonably spent upon the arbitration and also upon any travelling time; together with all expenses for travel, subsistence, hire of arbitration rooms, postage, FAX, Telex, cable, telephone, copying, recording, typing, transcribing, reports of experts and advisors, and any other like items, all chargeable at cost. Including an addition for VAT at the appropriate rate.
[*Which quoted rate shall be subject to review at six-monthly intervals from the date of this agreement.]
[#In the event that the arbitrator accepts the appointment prior to any agreement of fees and that the Claimant and Respondent have not subsequently agreed upon the fees, or any revision to the agreed fees, to be liable to pay a reasonable fee based upon the nature and complexity of the dispute; the degree of skill and specialised knowledge needed; the number and importance of the documents to be considered; the place and circumstances giving rise to the dispute and the location of the hearing and other work connected with the arbitration; the time spent upon the dispute; the monetary value of the dispute and the responsibility involved; together with all expenses for travel, subsistence, hire of arbitration rooms, postage, FAX, Telex, cable, telephone, copying, recording, typing, transcribing, reports of experts and advisers, and any other like items, all chargeable at cost. Including an addition for VAT at the appropriate rate.]

To be liable to take up the award of the arbitrator by payment of the arbitrator's fees and expenses within 14 days of being notified of the amount of such charges and that the award has been published.

That if an agreement is reached by the Claimant and Respondent on the matters in dispute, or on the termination or abandonment of the dispute before publication of the award, that they shall each be under an obligation to forthwith notify the arbitrator of such agreement, termination or abandonment and shall be liable to pay the proper charges of the arbitrator as may be due at that time. Such charges to include any reasonable charges in respect of the cancellation of reserved time and all committed expenses including costs in respect of accommodation, and other like items, which are no longer required.

Signed by:

[ON BEHALF OF] THE CLAIMANT

Date:

Signed by:*

[ON BEHALF OF] THE RESPONDENT

Date:

* Only applicable when both parties seek appointment.

I, ______________________________, having been appointed arbitrator, by ______________________________, in the above dispute, in accordance with the arbitration agreement and the above terms, hereby accept* the appointment.

Signed by:

THE ARBITRATOR

Date:

* (a) that in accepting the appointment the arbitrator relies upon the applicant's assertion that a genuine dispute does exists between the parties and that the dispute is subject to an arbitration agreement which provides for an appointment in the manner sought; (b) that the applicant shall, so soon as is practicable following the acceptance of this appointment by the arbitrator, submit proof of the applicant's assertions; and (c) that the applicant accepts full responsibility for all costs and fees incurred by the arbitrator and of any other party arising out of any aspects should there be no such dispute or no such arbitration agreement.

CASES REFERRED TO IN TEXT AND SELECTED BIBLIOGRAPHY

CASES

Aughton Ltd v. M.F. Kent Services Ltd, BLR 57, p. 6. (note 41)

Bremer Vulcan v. South India Shipping, [1981] 1 All ER 289. (notes 25, 46, 81, 104 & 157)

Courtney & Fairbairn Ltd v. Tolaini Brothers (Hotels) Ltd, [1975] 1 All ER 716. (note 55).

Harbutt's Plasticine Ltd v. Wayne Tank and Pump Co Ltd, [1970] 1 All ER 225. (note 107)

L'Office Cherifien des Phosphates v. Yamashita-Shinnihon Steamship Co. Ltd, The Boucraa, [1994] 1 All ER 20. (notes 25, 104 & 198)

Palacath Ltd v. Flanagan, [1985] 2 All ER 165. (note 154)

Photo Production Ltd v. Securicor Transport Ltd, [1980] 1 All ER 556. (note 107)

The K/S Norjarl A/S v. Hyundai Heavy Industries Co Ltd, [1991] 1 Lloyd's Report 268. (note 125)

The Moorcock, (note 113)

Taylor v. Yielding, (1912) 56 SJ 253. (note 154)

Tramountana v. Atlantic Shipping, [1978] 2 All ER 870. (note 59)

Wells v. Middleton, (1784) 1 Cox 112 124-5. (note 79)

[Some other cases are referred to as being included in the articles notes below.]

REFERENCE BOOKS & REPORTS

Russell on the Law of Arbitration, Anthony Walton Q.C., & Mary Vitoria, (London: Stevens & Sons, Twentieth Edition, 1982).

The Law and Practice of Commercial Arbitration in England, Sir Michael Mustill (now Lord Mustill) & Stewart Boyd Q.C., (London: Butterworth, Second Edition, 1989).

Handbook of Arbitration Practice, Ronald Bernstein Q.C., & Derek Wood Q.C., (London, Sweet & Maxwell, Second Edition, 1993).

[There are many other reference books about arbitration in England and Wales available for readers but, in the absence of listing them all, the author does not wish to select some as being more relevant than others. Like the book which you now read, they all have their place in seeking to explain and develop the business of arbitration.]

The Judge, Patrick Devlin, (Oxford: Oxford University Press, 1981).

Commercial Aspects of Trusts and Fiduciary Obligations, (Oxford: Clarendon Press, 1992).

Report on Arbitration, The Commercial Court Committee, Cmnd, July 1978.

[N.B. Between the *Report on Arbitration*, above, and the *Consultation Paper . . .*, below, there have been numerous reports issued by the DTI; the latter being what may be described as the "penultimate"; it takes stock - no doubt - of the intervening ones.]

A Consultation Paper on Draft Clauses and Schedules of an Arbitration Bill, Department of Trade and Industry, February 1994.

BY THE SAME AUTHOR

"Old Poe-face," *Arbitration,* Vol. 49, No. 3, February 1984, p. 266.

Arbitration - Recommendations & Survey, (Herne Bay: Ruthtrek, 1988) ISBN 0 9514295 0 7.

Précis of the Responses to Mr. Geoffrey King's address as Chairman of the Chartered Institute of Arbitrators, on the 7th June 1988, published March 1989, by the Chartered Institute of Arbitrators.

"Redefining terms of arbitration," *New Law Journal*, June 8 1990, p. 827.

"The judicial immunity of arbitrators," *New Law Journal*, May 11 1991, p. 633.

"Some Reflections on a Proposed New Arbitration Act," *(1991) 57, JCI Arb. 4*, p. 242.

"Terms of engagement," *New Law Journal*, November 29 1991, p. 1633.

"Another blunder hits the statute book," *New Law Journal*, October 16 1992, p. 1421.

"Arbitration; negligence and the arbitrator," *Tolley's Professional Negligence*, Vol. 9, No. 2, 1993, p. 70.

"Undertaking the undefinable," *New Law Journal*, June 25 1993, p. 928.

"The tribunal and the truth," *New Law Journal*, January 14 1994, p. 51.
